To:

....

From:

....

DEVOTIONS
from the FRONT PORCH

DEVOTIONS
from the FRONT PORCH

by STACY EDWARDS

THOMAS NELSON
Since 1798

CONTENTS

A ROCKING CHAIR

"Come to me, all you who are weary and burdened, and I will give you rest."

MATTHEW 11:28

We live in a society of stressed-out people. Stress affects young kids, college students, and adults; almost everyone seems touched by it. Then, in an attempt to ease the stress, we make it worse. We work harder. We work faster. We do more. We refuse to rest, and then we wonder why we're so exhausted. It's a vicious cycle.

Do you want to know who isn't stressed? Anyone currently sitting in a rocking chair. Try a little rocking on someone's front porch, and see what happens. You will rock your cares away, my friend.

Christ knew that life would be stressful. He didn't invite us to come to Him and have all of our problems solved. A quick fix or an end to the current struggle is not what our bodies need. He gives us what we often do not give ourselves: permission to rest.

We don't need to do one more load of laundry, or work longer or harder, or stay up later, or get up earlier. We need to rest, and Christ, in His wisdom, gives us permission to do just that. And not only does He offer rest, but He invites us to give our worries and burdens to Him.

We have permission to turn on the radio and dance in the kitchen. To laugh out loud. To simply breathe. We have permission to take a break from whatever is weighing us down. You and I have permission to rest, and there's no better place to rest than a front-porch rocking chair.

I am so thankful, Lord, that You know what I need. When I am weary and overwhelmed, help me remember to come to You for rest.

THE KITCHEN TABLE

While Jesus was having dinner at Matthew's house, many tax collectors and sinners came and ate with him and his disciples.

MATTHEW 9:10

Breaking bread with others is a special experience. Chances are, if a person is ill, has had a baby, or is new to the neighborhood, someone will show up with an offering of food. Many lasting friendships have been formed while sharing a chicken casserole or some pound cake.

The early believers understood this concept of community. They knew that life was not meant to be lived in isolation, but rather in interacting with and loving others well. They had witnessed the extraordinary way Christ loved, and it often involved dining with people. He feasted at Matthew's house, Martha's house, the seashore, and the Upper Room. He dined with His friends, His disciples, Pharisees, tax collectors, and lepers.

Jesus didn't withdraw from people or their pain. He was never too busy to be bothered by others' burdens. In fact, He invited them to step away from the busyness of life and share a meal with Him. As a result, the outcast felt as welcome at His dinner table as the disciple.

People are no different today than when Jesus walked the earth. We want to be seen and heard—to know we matter.

We are surrounded by hurting and lonely people who long for an invitation to break bread with us. They desire to be welcomed. When the coffee flows freely, people feel free to be themselves. If there happens to be a pound cake involved, well, that's just icing.

Lord, may I never be too busy to let someone know that he or she matters. May my kitchen table be a place where people are truly seen and heard. Open my eyes to those around me who need to be invited to break bread at my table.

SUNDAY
AFTERNOON NAPS

If you lie down, you will not be afraid; when you lie down, your sleep will be sweet.

PROVERBS 3:24 ESV

When you have children, sleep is the first thing you lose. As infants, they keep you up all hours of the night. Then they begin climbing into your bed in the middle of the night, kicking you in the back and stealing your covers. At some point, they finally sleep in their own beds, only to wake up at the crack of dawn requesting breakfast. Occasionally, however, something beautiful takes place on Sunday afternoon: a nap.

Whether it's on the couch, in a hammock, or on a blanket in the yard, a Sunday afternoon nap is a wise gift for a weary body. To close your eyes and snooze in the middle of the day seems positively decadent, which makes the sleep that much sweeter.

Solomon knew the importance of wisdom in a person's life. Of all the things that he could have requested from God, he asked for wisdom, and God granted it. Solomon also knew the benefits of wisdom in his life. Wisdom allows a person to walk in security and peace. A wise person is a source of life to those around her.

A foolish person makes foolish decisions and suffers the consequences—one of the first often being troubled sleep. When worry and regret weigh heavy on a person's mind, sleep proves elusive. A wise person, however, makes prayerful decisions, trusts God with the outcomes, and sleeps like it's Sunday afternoon.

I know what it's like, Lord, to endure sleepless nights.
Give me wisdom that I may always find rest in You.

BIRD-WATCHING

"Look at the birds of the air: they neither sow nor reap nor gather into barns, and yet your heavenly Father feeds them. Are you not of more value than they?"

MATTHEW 6:26 ESV

Although it may be hard to admit as they eat all the blueberries from the bushes in your yard, birds are fascinating creatures. They glide effortlessly through the air while singing the loveliest of songs. With a chirp and a hop, they go about their business as if they haven't a care in the world. It's difficult not to envy them.

The fact is, just like every living thing, birds must have food and water. They have and take care of babies; they need shade from the heat and shelter from the storm. So why aren't they scurrying and worrying? For the same reason you and I need not worry: the God who created them also cares for them.

Though they are truly lovely, we are far more valuable to God than the birds of the air. Our Creator is well aware of our every need, and He is able to meet each one of them. We add nothing to our lives when we worry—not minutes to our days or dollars to our bank accounts. Our worrying does not alter circumstances or alleviate problems.

Jesus knew that the tendency to worry was part of the human condition. During His earthly ministry, He addressed the issues of worry and anxiety on more than one occasion, and His message is clear: when we worry, we are in direct disobedience. We should, instead, take our cue from the birds. God always provides for them—even if He does so with the blueberries from the front yard.

*Forgive me, Lord, for my worrying ways. Help me to live
a little more like the birds and spend my days singing
of Your goodness and trusting in Your provision.*

CORNBREAD AND
BUTTERMILK

His delight is in the law of the LORD, and on
his law he meditates day and night.

PSALM 1:2 ESV

Some foods just naturally go together. Peanut butter and jelly. White beans and ham hocks. Chocolate and, well, anything. There's something unique, however, about the pairing of cornbread and buttermilk. According to my mama, "The longer it sets, the better it gets." The buttermilk must be poured generously so that it soaks into every morsel of cornbread.

The study of Scripture works much the same way. To delight in the law of the Lord is to partake of it generously and allow it to soak into our spirits. Our goal should not be to read as much as we can or as quickly as we can. Delight takes time as we soak up a verse, a phrase, or a word.

We can spend day and night worrying about all the what-ifs of this life, and we can hang on to a grudge for days without end. What if, however, the thing we dwelled on was the goodness of God? What if it wasn't worry but wonder that captivated us?

To meditate on Scripture is to read it over and over, allowing it to penetrate our minds. It is to read it slowly and out loud, emphasizing a different word with each reading. It is to ponder. To delight in the law of the Lord is to know that the longer it sets, the better it gets.

Lord, forgive me for treating the reading of Your Word as just another item on my to-do list. Teach me to delight in it daily and to meditate on it, no matter what my day holds.

GROCERY SHOPPING

One who is full loathes honey, but to one who is hungry everything bitter is sweet.

PROVERBS 27:7 ESV

Grocery shopping can be a tricky thing. If you shop with an empty stomach, you're likely to fill your cart with pecan twirls, sugary cereal, and day-old bakery doughnuts. Items from every shelf will call your name, causing you to spend far more than you anticipated. When you unload everything at home, you'll realize that you don't have a single proper meal. That's the danger of shopping while hungry—everything seems like a good idea.

It is far easier to shop logically on a full belly. You know what you need, and you aren't tempted by the call of the candy on aisle five. You're able to walk right by the frozen pizzas without a second glance. Perhaps you still accept the sample of sushi in the deli section, but the point is that when you're full, you're able to use better discretion when shopping.

When we spend time in prayer, Bible study, and communion with God, we are filled with the things of Him. We aren't interested in the things the world has to offer, no matter how tempting they may appear. But when we allow ourselves to get too busy to spend time with God, we wander out into the world with hungry hearts. Everything seems sweet and desirable.

We attempt to fill our emptiness with material possessions, the praise of others, and empty, mundane pursuits. Instead of feeling full and satisfied, we're left with the bitter aftertaste of disappointment and discouragement. It's a dangerous thing to go out into the world with a hunger inside. We must fill ourselves with His Word and with godly pursuits. Then we won't find ourselves unloading our groceries with buyer's remorse.

You, Lord, are the only thing that truly satisfies.
I desire to be filled with Your Spirit and Your truth
so that I don't crave the things of this world.

WIND CHIMES

Finally, brothers and sisters, whatever is true, whatever is noble, whatever is right, whatever is pure, whatever is lovely, whatever is admirable—if anything is excellent or praiseworthy—think about such things.

PHILIPPIANS 4:8

Life can get crazy loud. With work, friends, a spouse, children, church, household responsibilities, and a hundred other things going on, it can be challenging to carve out any peace and quiet.

Recently, I stepped out onto the porch to get a breath of fresh air, and I was instantly bombarded with noise. A barking dog next door. A neighbor mowing his lawn across the street. Cars driving up and down the road. My children laughing and playing in the yard. I was ready to turn around and go back inside, but then a soft wind began to blow.

Suddenly, I could hear the tinkling of the beautiful wind chimes that my husband had recently hung. I closed my eyes, and as I focused on the song of the wind chimes, other noises faded into the background. The noise disappeared because of what I chose to focus on.

The world is full of distractions, noises, and needs vying for our attention. These things seek space in our hearts and minds, making it easy to get overwhelmed and lose focus. Sometimes we need to stop and ask ourselves, *What is true? Noble? Right? Pure? Lovely? Admirable?* Then we must consciously choose to focus on those things and let the rest fade into the background.

Teach me, Lord, how to filter the many noises that surround me. Help me not to be so distracted by the "loud" things that I miss the delicate song of what truly matters.

HOUSEPLANTS

"Come, all you who are thirsty, come to the waters."

ISAIAH 55:1

If you don't water your plants regularly, they will die. Houseplants don't wither without reason. Water is necessary for plant life; it's essential for the human body as well. We can only last a short period of time without water. And, unfortunately, we cannot store it up for a future dry spell.

One of the symptoms of dehydration is fatigue. Without water, your body doesn't have what it needs to function, and you'll become weary and worn-out. Your spirit is much the same. Does life have you exhausted? Do you feel continually tired? It's possible that you are just plain thirsty. If so, the Lord said, "Come."

God knew that we would need Him, the Living Water, in order to survive in this barren land. Without Him pouring into us, we wither away like a neglected houseplant. We begin to shrivel up spiritually. But all we have to do to be replenished and refreshed is to come to Him.

Jeremiah 2:13 depicts God as a fountain and believers as cracked cisterns. When we immerse ourselves in God's Word, the water constantly flows over us. Sometimes we think we are good on our own, so we step away. The problem is that we are cracked cisterns. The moment we walk away from the fountain, the water begins to leak out. Soon we are dry, dehydrated, and weary.

Don't wait until you look like that forgotten potted plant in the corner of your living room. If you're feeling weary, worn-out, or tired, go to God. Drink freely and be refreshed.

Too often, Lord, I try to do it all on my own. I attempt to solve my own problems and heal my own hurts, and then I wonder why I feel weary. Fill me with the water of Your Word so I may be renewed once again.

SACRED SERVING

And he sat down and called the twelve. And he said to them, "If anyone would be first, he must be last of all and servant of all."

MARK 9:35 ESV

We all want to do big things for God, don't we? We watch someone go from obscurity to fame, and we think *that* is what it looks like to be used by God. We hear of someone overseas living among the poor, and suddenly our daily sacrifices don't feel so impressive. Sometimes it seems as if everyone else is doing bigger things for God.

We might be tempted to view our day-to-day tasks as mundane. Or we might analyze our responsibilities and deem some of them holy and some of them nuisances. If we listen to the world, we will begin to believe that the little acts of service don't matter and that everyone else is living a more glamorous life than we are.

The fact is, there are moments when we must wash the dishes, bathe the children, and clean up the spaghetti that the baby threw on the floor. In those moments, maybe our service *feels* menial. But sometimes the ministry is in the mess. The sacredness is in the serving.

We live in a world that respects first place. Whether it's a sporting event, a black Friday shopping line, or an airline boarding pass, we like to be in the front. Don't we all want just a little of the spotlight for ourselves? The problem is that these feelings of entitlement carry over into other areas of our lives. Perhaps we're only happy to serve as long as we get the accolades for doing so. But that isn't service at all. True servanthood begins in the heart. And we must decide if we want glamour for ourselves or glory for our Lord.

There are times, Lord, when I make serving You all about me. Forgive me for seeking glory for myself. Teach me the beauty of humility, and give me a servant's heart.

THE OLD AZALEA BUSH

"For I know the plans I have for you," declares the LORD, "plans to prosper you and not to harm you, plans to give you hope and a future."

JEREMIAH 29:11

As new homeowners, my husband and I had great intentions when it came to our landscaping. So, we bought an azalea bush. We chose the perfect spot, dug a hole, and planted it firmly in its new home. After a period of time, however, it became clear that the bush was not going to make it. Maybe the weeds were not pulled, or we didn't water it as often as needed. Regardless of the culprit, the bush died.

We did what any amateur gardeners would do: we dug it up and threw it out by the trash can. The plan was to carry it to the curb on trash day because there was no hope for that bush. But when trash day arrived, we discovered that next to the can was a beautiful, blooming azalea bush. We had given up too soon.

Jeremiah 29 is a letter written to people who had been taken into captivity. They weren't living the lives they had envisioned. It was as if someone had uprooted them from their carefully chosen spot in the sun and transplanted them into unfamiliar and undesirable territory. Yet, in that wasteland, Jeremiah wrote to them about the Lord's plans for their lives, about a future and a hope. In fact, they were instructed to grow in that foreign land.

Life rarely goes according to our plans. Circumstances change, and in an instant we can find ourselves in unfamiliar territory. It is not God's plan, however, that we wither away. Even when we are far from home, God's desire is that we continue to grow.

Thank You, Lord, that Your plans for me always include hope and a future. Help me to be the person You created me to be, no matter where You choose to place me.

BUNDT CAKES

*"For my thoughts are not your thoughts, neither are
your ways my ways," declares the Lord.*

Isaiah 55:8

Some things are hard to comprehend. The bundt cake is a perfect example. Do you know what the hole in the center of a bundt cake is called? I don't either. Here's what it should be called: wasted space where there should be one more piece of cake. Now, I totally get that it is a very pretty dessert. I'm just saying that there's room for more cake.

Bundt cakes are not the only source of confusion in this world. Every day we see things that we do not understand. Hungry children and sick parents. Job losses and pink slips. Friends who betray and spouses who walk away. The world can be an overwhelming place.

So many things are beyond our comprehension. Our finite minds were not made to understand all of the intricacies of God's creation. Even Solomon, with all of his wisdom, admitted that there was much that he did not understand (Proverbs 30:18–19).

Accepting that we cannot understand everything is how we are able to make it through certain seasons. When we look at a situation and cannot make sense of it at all, it would be terribly frustrating if we thought that we were seeing the whole picture. We can find comfort in knowing that much more is going on. In the midst of our confusion, we can know that God is up to something bigger, and we can trust Him completely.

*Sometimes I'm confused by my circumstances. I fear what
I do not understand. Help me, Lord, to remember that there
is much that I don't see. Teach me to trust You more.*

A TRIP TO TOWN

For the Scripture says, "Whoever believes in
Him will not be disappointed."

Romans 10:11 NASB

Not too long ago I joined my husband on a work trip to Chicago. We had not traveled together in years, and although we did take our newborn with us, it was still quite exciting to get away. We pulled out of the driveway on a sunny Thursday morning with classic country music on the radio and lattes in our hands. Taking back roads, with the baby sleeping the entire way, the drive was idyllic.

By the time Saturday rolled around, however, the hotel room toilet had overflowed, the baby had cried nonstop, and my husband had come down with food poisoning. Did I mention it was also pouring rain? I had been envisioning peaceful mornings with my Bible and coffee, afternoons watching television, and evenings in the city with my man. What I had, instead, was a hotel room with sketchy Wi-Fi that reeked of dirty diapers, leftover pizza, and misery.

Hello, disappointment.

Disappointment comes when we don't get what we expect or when something unpleasant happens that we do *not* expect. Unfortunately, life is full of the unexpected and is, therefore, often full of disappointment. Thankfully, there's good news.

God is always who He says He is, and we can expect Him to do what He says He will do. He will never disappoint us.

Life can be hard; that's just a fact. Sometimes we're expecting a weekend getaway, and we end up with food poisoning. But God is still God. We can choose to wallow in our disappointment, or we can believe in the One who never disappoints.

This world promises things that it can never deliver. If my hope is in anything other than You, Lord, I am destined for disappointment. Please help me to place all my hope in You.

CHECKING THE LOCKS

Don't worry about anything.

PHILIPPIANS 4:6 HCSB

It seems positively unthinkable in this day and age, but there was a time when folks didn't lock their doors. People slept with their windows open and enjoyed an evening breeze without a second thought. Nowadays, you don't just lock your doors; you check and double-check the locks before going to bed. Every potential entrance to the home is made as secure as possible to protect against unwanted visitors in the middle of the night.

If you're like me, occasionally after you've gone to bed, you will hear a noise and feel obligated to recheck everything. This world gives us plenty of things to be concerned about. With the news full of stories of crime and concern, we're convinced that there are things we should be worried about.

Only you know the specific worries that keep you up at night. Perhaps it's a security issue that has you up checking the locks. Maybe it's a family issue or a financial concern. No matter what you're worrying about, one thing is always true: your worry falls under the category of "anything."

The instruction in Scripture is "don't worry about *anything*." Family, finances, health, personal safety—it all falls under the same heading. We can trust God with our "anything" because He has promised to supply our every need (Philippians 4:19). That family, financial, health, or safety concern is taken care of in the "every need" category. We don't have to worry because God has already got it covered.

So lock your doors, and go to sleep. The Lover of your soul can handle the night shift.

I know that my tendency to worry is sin, Lord. I worry because I know there are things out of my control, and I forget that nothing is out of Your control. Forgive me for the times I have failed to take You at Your Word.

CURB APPEAL

A happy heart makes the face cheerful.

PROVERBS 15:13

Maybe it's wrong to judge a book by its cover, but folks still do it. The same is true for a house. Whether you are buying or selling a home, curb appeal matters. Overgrown lawns do not sell homes. That gutter up in the tree may be an interesting conversation piece, but Susie-home-buyer is not going to be interested. If the outside of the home is unappealing, most potential buyers will not be willing to step inside and give it a chance.

The fact is true for more than just houses. Sometimes we Christians are known more for what we are against than anything else. We can be quick to speak the truth in opposition to something, but too often we forget to do it in love. We must remember that our conversations are to be full of grace (Colossians 4:6). As Christ-followers, we need to learn to be passionate without being off-putting. The solution can be as simple as a smile.

Have you ever passed someone in the grocery store and had her smile at you? When someone appears friendly, you're more likely to want to get to know her. A cheerful face matters. Now, I'm not suggesting that you be phony or walk around with a goofy grin all day, but try to display a friendly demeanor.

A cheerful face tells passersby that you are approachable. And when you are able to exude joy even in the midst of difficulties, it causes people to ponder the source of that joy. So, remember: your smile is your curb appeal. It tells people that there's something inside worth checking out.

Lord, forgive me for being quick to give my opinion and forgetting to do it in love. Help me to show, on the outside, the joy You have given me on the inside.

WASTE NOT, WANT NOT

*I want you to know, brothers and sisters, that what has happened
to me has actually served to advance the gospel.*

PHILIPPIANS 1:12

Every experienced cook knows that nothing in the kitchen should go to waste. Is there a whole chicken in the Crock-Pot? The meat is going to be eaten. The bones will be used to give flavor to a soup on another day. The drippings will be saved and turned into a homemade broth. Nothing gets thrown away. Ask anyone raised in the South, and she'll tell you about her grandma's jar of bacon grease. That's the stuff green beans are made of, my friend.

Older generations who have known what it means to do without will also tell you that nothing should be wasted. Although it may not be immediately recognizable, everything has a purpose. Even pain in a person's life has a purpose. In Philippians, Paul gives two purposes behind pain.

First, your pain can be used to advance the gospel (Philippians 1:12–13). When you hurt, the world is watching to see if your mountaintop faith works in the valley. Paul, even in the midst of suffering, was quick to point others to Christ. He did not seek pity for his circumstances; instead, he offered praise for his Savior.

Second, your pain can be used to encourage fellow believers (Philippians 1:14). When fellow believers see you continue to praise God in the midst of pain, it gives them strength to do the same. Because of Paul's faith during his imprisonment, others felt empowered to preach the gospel.

The fact is, there is no avoiding pain. In a broken world, sometimes life hurts. But you don't have to let the pain be in vain. Allow your suffering to advance the gospel and encourage others.

> *Forgive me, Lord, for the times when I have chosen*
> *the route of self-pity instead of praise. Remind me,*
> *even in my pain, that the world is watching and they*
> *need to see You. Don't let me waste my pain.*

GRANDMA'S LILAC TREE

Our lives are a Christ-like fragrance rising up to God.

2 CORINTHIANS 2:15 NLT

My grandma had a lilac tree that covered the entire side of her three-story home. Yet, I never realized how impressive it truly was until, years later, I attempted to grow my own. The little stick that I planted never turned into the massive purple beauty I remembered.

Though Grandma's tree certainly was a beautiful sight, the real gift of that lilac tree was its scent. We would pull into her driveway, and when the blossoms were in bloom, I could smell the fragrance before I ever got out of the car. I would sit on her porch, and when the wind blew just the right way, the little blossoms would fly through the air and land right in my lap. Years later, every time I smell lilacs, I think of Grandma.

I have often wondered what a Christlike fragrance would smell like. Perhaps it's the smell of a burnt offering or of incense burning in the temple. Possibly it's the smell of the spices used on Christ's body before it went into the tomb or the ointment Mary poured on Him in worship. Though I do not know the exact aroma, I do know what causes it.

We remind God of His Son when we offer our lives as living sacrifices. We bear a beautiful resemblance to Christ when we love as He loved. When we extend grace and forgiveness, it's a familiar scent to the Father. On our own, we do not have a pleasing aroma. However, when we are in Christ, we take on His fragrance. We should live in such a way that when God smells us, He thinks of Jesus.

God, I am so thankful that when You look at me, You see Jesus' sacrifice on my behalf. Help me to live in such a way as to bring a Christlike fragrance before You.

BLANCHING YOUR VEGETABLES

Preach the word; be prepared in season and out of season.

2 TIMOTHY 4:2

You may think that in a small town, the worst thing one could be known as is a gossip. Maybe folks are still talking about that time you fell into the punch bowl at Sally Benson's baby shower. Perhaps you are sick of hearing about the time your child knocked over the Christmas tree in the downtown department store. Plenty of ways abound to embarrass oneself in a town where everyone knows everyone else's business.

In certain parts of the country, however, not blanching your vegetables will make you the topic of rocking-chair gossip on porches all over town. Folks will begin questioning everything they thought they knew about you. Everyone knows that a woman who doesn't blanch her vegetables cannot be trusted.

The blanching of vegetables prior to canning ensures full flavor and color in the future and enables them to survive storage. For instance, canned blanched vegetables taste fresh from the farm when added to a chicken casserole months later. Blanching prepares the vegetables for future use. Without this process, a cook runs the risk of limp, bland ingredients, and no one needs that. The preparation on the front end is essential.

Similarly, spending time in prayer and Bible study is essential for preparing your heart for the future. Paul instructed Timothy to be prepared in season and out of season. In other words, he needed to be prepared in advance. Every believer must do the same. We must do the work each day to be prepared so that when the hard times come, our hearts are ready to trust God and apply His truth in our situation.

We need to prepare our hearts now for difficult seasons to come. Otherwise, we run the risk of a limp, bland faith, and no one needs that.

I do not want to be caught unprepared, Lord. Teach me the discipline of daily time with You. Fill my heart with Your truths that will carry me through hard seasons.

STORM CLOUDS

"Watch out for false prophets. They come to you in sheep's clothing, but inwardly they are ferocious wolves. By their fruit you will recognize them."

MATTHEW 7:15–16

Whether you are a farmer tending your crops, a family planning a vacation, or a mama who desperately wants her kids to play outside, people who care about the weather watch the clouds. Some clouds mean pleasant weather, while others indicate an impending storm. And certain clouds are a sign that the rain may stick around for a while. Whatever your plans for the day, it's important to be able to recognize the warning signs of a coming storm.

Jesus warned that there would be false prophets. There will be those who pretend to be His, but, in actuality, they are not. How are Christ's followers supposed to be able to distinguish the true prophets from the false ones? We have to be able to recognize the warning signs.

Those who follow Christ have the fruit of the Spirit: love, joy, peace, patience, goodness, gentleness, kindness, faithfulness, and self-control. When someone exhibits these qualities, it's evidence that they're walking in the Spirit. Likewise, those who are in opposition to Christ have fruit of their own. To properly discern true from false, one must observe the fruit being produced.

Much as clouds warn of a coming storm, Scripture gives clear warnings against a variety of dangers believers will encounter. Proverbs warns against gossip, lying, and many other activities. Jesus' parables warn against being disobedient and ill prepared. Warnings are everywhere. It doesn't take a meteorologist to recognize a storm cloud, and you don't have to be a seminary graduate to recognize the fruit of a false prophet.

Thank You, Lord, for loving us enough to provide warnings in Your Word. Help me to recognize the warning signs of dangerous behavior and of false prophets.

A PORCH SWING

Make it your ambition to lead a quiet life.

1 Thessalonians 4:11

Her name was Gertrude, but her friends called her Gertie—a downright Southern name for someone from the hills of West Virginia. She was a grandmother to many, and though she has been gone for some time, quite a few folks still recall fond memories concerning her old porch swing. Many a grandchild spent summer days on that swing, far away from grown-up conversations.

Symbolic of the rhythm of a godly life, a porch swing is slow but consistent. There's no rush or hurry to its sway. In fact, if you've ever tried to swing high and fast on a porch swing, then you've surely discovered that it rocks unsteadily and loses its rhythm altogether.

Christ modeled a slow-paced life, often withdrawing to quiet, secluded places to pray. And He instructed His followers to do the same. He did not rush from one miracle to the next. Because He was unhurried, the woman with the issue of blood was able to reach out and touch the hem of His robe. Christ took the time to truly connect with the people around Him, and, because of that, He noticed Zacchaeus perched high in a tree.

Surely there are times for the excitement of a monster amusement park swing ride or the noise and activity of a playground. But for the day-in and day-out of life, the quiet of a good, old-fashioned porch swing is just fine.

Lord, teach me the beauty of an unhurried life. Help me to step away from the noise and into the quiet so I can better hear Your voice. I don't want to look back and regret the way I rushed through this life. May I learn to live the quiet life that You modeled so well.

FENCES

Now all the believers were together and held all things in common.

ACTS 2:44 HCSB

When people begin compiling their must-haves for a new home, a fenced-in yard may be included on the list. For some, perhaps it's because they have pets or small children who need a safe place to roam. But for many of us, the fence reflects a desire for privacy. Fences allow us to live among people while still controlling how often we interact with them. At the very least, they serve as a divider.

A fence is a way of saying, "I am responsible for this, and you are responsible for that." The old proverb says that good fences make good neighbors. A fence, however, doesn't really *make* anything. If you think about it, a fence simply separates. Whether it's cheap chain link or fancy wrought iron, the purpose of a fence is to delineate where you end and your neighbor begins.

Early believers wouldn't have understood the concept of fencing off one's personal property. They held everything in common. They sold all of their possessions, compiled the money, and gave to each person as needs arose. It was community in the purest sense of the word. Though they may have lived in separate homes, they did life together.

Now, no one is suggesting that you do away with your fence. After all, nothing makes loving thy neighbor more difficult than when thy neighbor's dog uses your lawn as a public restroom. Sometimes fences can be a really good thing!

However, as Christ-followers, we aren't meant to live in isolation. We are to be concerned with the well-being of our neighbors, seeking ways to serve them and to love them. We should spend time getting to know and caring for the people on the other side of the fence.

Lord, forgive me for being overly consumed with my little place in the world. Help me to love my neighbors well.

FAMILY RULES

But the fruit of the Spirit is love, joy, peace, patience, kindness, goodness, faithfulness, gentleness, self-control; against such things there is no law.

GALATIANS 5:22–23 ESV

We find security in knowing who we are and where we come from. In our home, we have our "family rules" posted on the wall. These rules serve as a reminder to us, and to anyone entering our home, of who we are as a family. We are thankful; we dream big and laugh loudly; we respect ourselves and others. When someone crosses the threshold of our home, they can expect to be greeted with kindness, coffee, and a whole lot of kids.

These family rules also serve as a plumb line by which we can measure our attitudes and actions. If there is a relational issue, those involved can stop and ask one another, "What is the point of this tension? Is there a family rule that is being broken?" In most instances, a simple reminder is all that's needed to correct a behavior.

The fruit of the Spirit mentioned in Scripture could be considered a Christian's family rules, describing who we are as Christ-followers. If we are abiding in the Spirit, then we will exhibit the appropriate fruit. Our actions will be guided by love. Our lives will display joy, peace, and patience. Our relationships will be marked by kindness, goodness, faithfulness, and gentleness. We will handle ourselves with self-control, doing all these things because it is who we are as a people.

When we find ourselves in a situation wrought with strife or tension, we can look to this passage in Galatians and discern which piece of the fruit is lacking. As we determine which characteristic is missing, we can ask God to restore it.

> *Lord, thank You for making it very clear who I am in You. Thank You for an understandable set of family rules so that I can honor You with my actions.*

EASTER EGGS

"You will seek me and find me when you seek me with all your heart."

JEREMIAH 29:13

Every spring in yards across the country, parents and grandparents get busy hiding Easter eggs. There are real dyed eggs and plastic eggs filled with candy and other wonderful surprises. The eggs are carefully hidden under leaves and up on tree branches. Once everything is in place, the kids are released to see how many they can find.

At first, the egg hunt is easy and fun. Some of the eggs placed out in the open are discovered quickly. There are giggles and squeals as children find eggs on porch steps and sidewalks. There comes a point, however, when the hunt becomes something resembling work. The children must move and lift things and be intentional in their search for eggs. No longer out in the open, the remaining Easter eggs are hidden under bushes and behind fences. A searcher must be a little more diligent in the quest.

Finding God can seem like an Easter egg hunt. When times are good, we see God everywhere. Much like the eggs placed in the open, He is easy to find in the random card from a friend or an unexpected windfall of money. We sense His presence in the good news and sunny days. At other times, however, there are cloudy days and bad news. In those moments, we must be intentional about seeking Him.

When the diagnosis isn't good, we must search a little harder. When the wound goes deep, we must seek a little more. It isn't always easy, but it is worth the search. God is there in the hard times just as He is in the good times. Much like the hidden Easter egg, He is always there waiting to be found.

Thank You, Lord, for Your promised presence. Your Word assures me that if I seek You with all my heart, I will find You. No matter my circumstance, I know that You are with me.

STRAWBERRY PRETZEL SALAD

No one can lay any foundation other than the one
already laid, which is Jesus Christ.

1 CORINTHIANS 3:11

I f you've ever been to a church social or potluck, there's a good chance you've enjoyed a few bites of strawberry pretzel salad. If, by some sad twist of fate, you're not familiar with this dish, you need to know a few things: There is salty. There is sweet. There is cream cheese. And this combo is every bit as delightful as it sounds.

The layers of this dish are more than pretty; they serve a purpose and must be added in the proper order. First, a foundation of crushed pretzels completely covers the bottom and sides of the dish. If the foundation is not handled properly, then the cream cheese and strawberry layers will seep down into and under the pretzel layer, creating a soggy crust. And believe me, you do *not* want to show up at Wednesday night supper with a soggy crust on your strawberry pretzel salad.

Whether it's a home, a dessert, or a life, the foundation is crucial to everything that follows. As Christ-followers, our foundation is Jesus. Any attempt to build a life on financial gain, professional success, or the praise of others will result in ruin. A worldly foundation is shaky and unable to withstand the storms of life. Your popularity will be of no comfort when you have more month than money or when someone you love is ill. Only Christ will remain faithful and steadfast. Only He can carry you safely through any storm. Jesus is the only firm foundation.

You, Lord, are the only sure foundation. Whatever
I may gain or accomplish in this life will not
amount to anything unless I put You first.

RAINY DAYS

He covers the heavens with clouds; he prepares rain for
the earth; he makes grass grow on the hills.

PSALM 147:8 ESV

As a child, you likely considered a rainy day to be a ruined day. Perhaps as an adult, however, a good summer storm makes your heart happy. It's easy to lose yourself in the sound of a steady rain. Often a nice downpour allows a person to set aside whatever he or she may have had planned and simply enjoy the rain and consider the way God cares for His creation.

The rain falling from the heavens to the thirsty earth below is a visible reminder of the way Jesus is Living Water to our thirsty souls. We may not realize what we need until the rain begins to fall, but God knows and is prepared. He knows how to make grass grow on the hills and how to refresh weary souls (Jeremiah 31:25).

So, when the rainy days come, don't consider them to be ruined days. Accept them as a gift. Sit on the porch, close your eyes, and listen to His love rain down on you.

Thank You, Lord, for bringing times of refreshment to my
soul. Thank You for the way You care for Your creation. When
my soul is dry, I only need for You to rain down on me.

THE DOORBELL

"And when you pray, do not keep on babbling like pagans, for they think they will be heard because of their many words."

MATTHEW 6:7

Someone should really teach a class on doorbell etiquette. Some folks seem to be under the impression that if one ring of the bell is nice, then three will be crazy fun for everyone. Here's the thing, though. When you ring someone's doorbell, he or she probably heard you the first time. Still, just to be on the safe side, a second ring is appropriate.

However, if no one comes to the door after the second ring, there are a couple of possibilities to consider. The first is that someone is home but doesn't want to open the door. If you think this might be the case, stop ringing the doorbell. The other possibility is that no one is home. I have watched a salesman ring the neighbor's doorbell multiple times before proceeding to walk around to the back door and ring the doorbell there, only to return to the front porch again. It just didn't matter how many times he rang that bell; there was no one home to hear it.

Jesus' description of a pagan's prayer was much like the persistent salesman. It didn't matter how many words the pagan used; his prayer was not going to be heard. Like so many other religious practices of the day, it was all a show. Jesus was not placing a word limit on prayer; rather, He was emphasizing the sincerity of the prayer.

The Lord is always attuned to the hearts of His people. He is already listening before the first breath of a prayer is uttered, as if He opened the door before you even had a chance to ring the doorbell.

*Thank You, Lord, that Your ears are always
open to my pleas. May my words be few and my
prayers be more listening than speaking.*

SIDEWALK CHALK

Why, you do not even know what will happen tomorrow. What is your life? You are a mist that appears for a little while and then vanishes.

JAMES 4:14

Sidewalks decorated by children with chalk are a common sight in most neighborhoods. From your porch, you can see the careful selection of colors and the great attention to detail. Little ones put a lot of time and effort into creating something that will be faded by the sun or washed away by the rain. Stick figures, hopscotch patterns, and other works of art are here today and gone tomorrow.

Many of the things we spend our time and attention on are as fleeting as a child's sidewalk chalk art. We spend precious moments focusing on trivial pursuits that only provide momentary pleasures. We plan for tomorrow while wasting today. The problem is that we are not promised tomorrow. All we can be absolutely certain of is the present moment.

In chapter 6 of Matthew's gospel, Jesus instructs believers not to worry about tomorrow. James reiterated this important truth in his book. Our lives are only a mist. We need to focus our attention on the things that make a difference in eternity. Financial gain, popularity, and the praise of men are like works of art made with sidewalk chalk. Though pleasant in the moment, they are only temporary. One mistake, illness, or change of fortune, and it could all go away in an instant.

So, what are you focusing on? Where are you spending the majority of your time, finances, and energy? Are you working on something permanent, or could a little rain wash it all away?

The world makes so many things appear important, Lord. Give me discernment about how I spend my time and energy. I want to keep my gaze on You.

DAYDREAMING

Many are the plans in the mind of a man, but it is
the purpose of the LORD that will stand.

PROVERBS 19:21 ESV

A front porch lends itself to daydreaming. Several years ago my husband and I felt the Lord leading us toward a certain area of ministry, which just happened to be really close to the beach. We sat on the porch, day after day, dreaming of how we were going to suffer for the Lord with our toes in the sand. (Someone has to do it.)

Now, mind you, it was not all about us. We were going to get a little condo with an ocean view and share it with our friends, blessing others with our little beachfront beauty. We were really generous with our daydreaming!

As it turned out, our plans did not line up with what God had in mind for our family at this time. God began closing some doors and opening others, and we found ourselves nowhere near the ocean and in no position to buy beachfront property.

Sometimes God gives us a little glimpse of a picture, and we think we know exactly what He's doing. We run on ahead, dreaming and making plans. The reality is, however, that we know very little about the ways of the Lord. While it is okay to make plans, we need to allow room for God's greater purposes.

My husband and I are still daydreamers, but occasionally we feel ourselves getting a little ahead of God. In those moments, we remind ourselves of the condo that never was.

I love to plan my life, Lord. I think I know what I need, and sometimes I take steps in the wrong direction. Thank You for loving me enough to stop me before I go too far.

YARD SALES

But he was stunned at this demand, and he went away
grieving, because he had many possessions.

MARK 10:22 HCSB

A person is never fully aware of how attached she is to her stuff until strangers are digging through it in her front yard. It's hard not to be offended when someone offers you only a quarter for that treasured possession you cherished through all of your middle school years. It is probably safe to say that we place a little too much value on things.

Each year hundreds of people make the decision to spread their entire lives out on folding tables. They attempt to assign prices to unworn clothing and unused toasters, knowing that one of two outcomes will take place. Someone is going to load the items into a car and drive away; or no one will consider the items worthy of purchasing, and they will be left behind. There is a little heartache either way.

The rich young ruler desired eternal life, and he took pride in being a keeper of the commandments. On the outside, he seemed to be everything that a Christ-follower should be. But Jesus, knowing the young man's heart, revealed what truly held his devotion. Jesus told him to sell everything he owned in exchange for treasures in heaven, which caused the man to walk away in sadness.

It is easy enough to accumulate stuff. If we aren't careful, however, our things begin to take up as much space in our hearts as they do in our homes. We may find ourselves holding a little too tightly to the things of this world. Although we may try to justify this, the reality is, it is idolatry.

Do we love our stuff a little too much? Maybe it's time for a yard sale.

The desire of my heart, Lord, is to hold loosely to the things of this world. Help me to make You my true treasure, for possessions are a poor substitute.

SUN TEA

*"But when you pray, go into your room and shut the door
and pray to your Father who is in secret."*

MATTHEW 6:6 ESV

Growing up, it wasn't uncommon to see a large jar of tea sitting in the sun on Mama's front porch. A quick Internet search would reveal a popular food site that lists twelve steps for making sun tea. Count 'em—twelve! But do you know what you need to make sun tea? Sun, water, and tea bags. That's it. It's quite possible that we've made things far too complicated.

Prayer has become the same way. Type the words "how to pray" into a search engine, and you'll get more than 180 million results in less than half a second. You'll find articles and books to study, suggestions of classes to take, and more how-to blog posts than one person can ever get around to reading. A person could spend every waking moment trying to figure out how to pray and never get around to actually praying.

The disciples who followed Jesus during His earthly ministry witnessed His devotion to prayer as He regularly retreated to privately talk to God. When Jesus instructed His disciples on the practice of prayer, He didn't teach them a *PRAY* acrostic. He didn't list seven ways to get closer to God. There was nothing complicated in Jesus' approach to prayer.

Go into your room.

Shut the door.

Pray.

Prayer is unhurried. It's uncomplicated. It's refreshing. Kind of like a nice, tall glass of sun tea.

Lord, thank You for modeling a consistent prayer life. Help me to follow Your recipe for prayer and not the complicated concept the world offers.

KEEPING UP WITH THE JONESES

Each one should test their own actions. Then they can take pride in themselves alone, without comparing themselves to someone else.

GALATIANS 6:4

Are you ever tempted to look at the neighbors and compare yourself to them? Perhaps from your perch on the porch, their lives look pretty great. You see them open their car doors, and trash doesn't even fall out. Meanwhile, you could feed a small country with the discarded french fries and cereal remnants in the floor of your van. The last time you used the restroom at their house, it felt like a trip to the spa. It's a good day if yours has some toilet paper left on the roll.

The enemy wants you to think that the neighbors have it easier than you. He wants to convince you that they are better than you. Satan doesn't want people to join together in community. He doesn't want open, honest relationships. He would much rather you isolate yourself and feel alone. The enemy wants you to believe that no one else deals with the things you deal with at home. But it's all a lie.

No one is living a perfect life. Everyone has heartache, drama, and sleepless nights. You don't need to compare yourself to someone else in order to feel good about yourself. If you're doing the very best you can, then take pride in each day. It doesn't matter if their children always wear matching outfits and your kids don't even wear matching socks. At the end of the day, it doesn't mean a thing. Don't allow insecurity and the comparison game to keep you from loving your neighbor. And chances are, they're sitting on their porch thinking that your life looks pretty great.

I have played the timid, insecure person for too long, Lord.
I have listened to the enemy's lies and allowed him to shame
me into isolation. Give me the boldness to be real with
others so that they feel the freedom to be real too.

SPRING CLEANING

Repent, then, and turn to God, so that your sins may be wiped out, that times of refreshing may come from the Lord.

ACTS 3:19

There are different levels of cleaning the home. There's the kind of cleaning you do on a regular basis: wash the dishes, do the laundry, make the beds, rewash the laundry that sat in the machine overnight. Then there's the quick cleaning you do for unexpected company. (This is when you shove toys into closets, light a candle, and close all of the bedroom doors!)

During a certain time of year, however, cleaning takes on a whole new meaning. There's no specific date on the calendar for this chore; you just wake up one morning, and you know it's spring cleaning time. It's time to begin to deal with all those tasks that you've been ignoring for too long.

During this deep cleaning, ceiling fans are finally dusted, curtains are taken down and washed, and the windows are opened to allow the breeze to blow through your home. Closets get reorganized, and furniture gets rearranged. Long-neglected tasks are completed, and the entire home seems fresh and new.

When it comes to our spiritual lives, it's easy to get caught up in the day-to-day kind of cleaning. We do just what is necessary for the immediate maintenance of our faith. If we aren't careful, however, we let some tasks go undone. Dust bunnies begin to accumulate. We need a spiritual spring cleaning.

We must seek the Lord and ask Him to reveal any sin that may be making itself at home in our hearts. When it is revealed, we can repent and turn from it. Then God will make our spirits fresh and new.

Lord, sometimes I get caught up in the day-to-day tasks and fail to address the deeper issues affecting my spirit. Reveal to me, Father, the areas where I need to repent so that Your refreshing breeze may blow.

THE SIMPLE LIFE

Then He said to them, "Go into all the world and
preach the gospel to the whole creation."

MARK 16:15 HCSB

Many of us are seeking simplicity. We cook simple meals and design simple homes. We homeschool and homestead. We limit activities to simplify our calendars. In order to cut back, we say no. We live with less, posting pictures of our simple lives all over social media. Yet, if we're honest, nothing about life seems simple.

It's okay to long for a simple life. Many times in Scripture, Jesus told His followers to be still and to seek solitude. Yet, too many of us have confused a simple life with an easy life, and if we're honest, an easy life is really what we want. But life doesn't work that way. Family is complicated. Ministry is messy. Parenting is exhausting. Loving people well can make a body weary. We see loss and brokenness everywhere; no matter how hard we try, nothing is easy.

But God never offered His followers an easy life. Christ never said, "Pick up your easy life and follow Me." His instructions for our lives, however, were simple.

Go to every corner of creation.
Proclaim the good news to everyone in the world.
Pick up your cross.
Look after orphans.
Take care of widows.
Love your neighbors.
Don't forget your enemies. Love them too.

Feed the hungry.
Clothe the naked.
Proclaim freedom to the prisoner.
Love.
Love.
Love.

All simple instructions, though none of them is easy. But we really can't say that no one warned us. God said to go everywhere. Paul said to expect some pain. Jesus warned that the world would hate us like it hated Him. Being a Christian isn't easy, but it truly is the simple life.

I say I long for a simple life, but often what I am really
seeking is an easy life. Give me the strength, Lord, to
seek You and let You do with my life what You will.

PLANTING FLOWERS

*And let us not grow weary of doing good, for in due
season we will reap, if we do not give up.*

GALATIANS 6:9 ESV

Growing up in my house, the first task of spring was the purchasing of
flowers for the front flower bed. My father took this job very seriously.
There had to be an equal number of each type of plant, in a variety of colors.
They were not planted willy-nilly, meaning that my father would take out his
tape measure and find the exact spot where each plant should be placed.

After he had placed the still-potted plants in perfectly spaced rows, we
would all stand on one side of the flower bed and then the other, tilting our
heads this way and that way. Finally, when it was determined that everything
was just as he wanted it, we dug the holes. Planting flowers with my dad was
not for the faint of heart!

Although there is not a right or wrong way to plant flowers, the fact is, we
had the prettiest flower bed on the street. Not once did my dad ever regret the
work he put into it.

That's the way God intended many things in life. Work comes before the
reward. It takes effort and sweat and getting our hands dirty. Hard work and
sacrifice are required. All of the work is done in expectation of the appropriate
desired result in due time. If we were to give up at any point, we would never
know the beauty that would have been ours to enjoy.

*Teach me to endure, Lord. Give me the strength and discipline to carry
on so that I, in due season, may reap the rewards of a life lived for You.*

BREAKFAST

In the morning, Lord, you hear my voice; in the morning
I lay my requests before you and wait expectantly.

PSALM 5:3

It's long been taught that breakfast is the most important meal of the day. Whether you prefer something quick or a sit-down meal, most people know that eating a healthy meal in the morning gives the body needed nutrients and energy. But if that's the case, why do so many of us skip it? We deny our bodies what they need, and then we wonder why we're drained and unable to focus later in the day.

Spending time with the Lord in the morning is like breakfast for our spirits. Not knowing what a day may hold, it is important to begin the day with our focus on things eternal. No law or commandment says that believers must have prayer in the morning. The example is set, however, all throughout Scripture. Job rose early each morning to pray for his children (Job 1:5). David sought God in the morning (Psalm 5:3). Jesus got up very early to pray (Mark 1:35).

As believers, we need to start our day with full bellies and full spirits. Taking time to connect with God in the morning sets our priorities for the rest of the day and prepares us for whatever may come our way.

If you've ever been running late and thought, *I'll grab a bite to eat later*, you know that often doesn't happen. You end up filling yourself with the wrong things because you are starving and desperate. Spending time with God can go the same way. If you think, *Oh, I'll do that a little later*, it may not happen at all and the enemy will put other things in your path.

We must commit to starting our day off right, filling our bellies and our spirits before rushing off to face what the day has in store.

Forgive me, Lord, for not giving You the first fruits of my time and energy. Remind me to stop and connect with You before going out into the world. Fill me with Your Spirit so that I exude You for the rest of the day.

LIFE STORY

Nothing in all creation is hidden from God's sight.

Hebrews 4:13

We don't get to choose our story. If we could, wouldn't we all choose the one where life is easy and each day is sunshine and sweet tea? Wouldn't we wish happy endings for ourselves and everyone we love? But it isn't our choice to make. We can, however, choose God and choose to walk bravely wherever He leads.

The reality is that life is hard for everyone. No one gets to choose the easy life. Life can be difficult for you, for me, and for the lady with the tired eyes in the cereal aisle. That waiter who just poured your coffee may be struggling to make ends meet. Illness, job loss, family hurts, and soul wounds visit all of us, and some leave the forever kind of scars. But we can still choose God and trust Him with our story.

Our story, in Him, is one of letting go. We let go of the notion that we are the heroes in our stories. We realize, instead, that He is the hero, and He came to save us. So we push through trials, devastations, and heartaches. We may not have chosen our circumstances, but we are smitten with the Savior who urges us onward.

We offer up our lives to the Author of our faith story, knowing that, in time, all will be redeemed and restored. We can trust that if we could see what He sees, we would say, "Yes, Lord, this is the story I would have chosen for myself."

Sometimes, Lord, I look at my life and think that I would have done things differently. I just don't see what You see. I know that nothing is hidden from Your sight, and so I trust You with my life.

SCREENED-IN PORCH

"As it is, you do not belong to the world, but I have chosen you out of the world."

JOHN 15:19

Advertising folks know how to make a hot summer day seem like a little piece of paradise. Perfectly tanned people sport stylish summer hats. Everyone glistens, but no one sweats. Yes, in magazine and television land, everyone loves summer. There's just one problem with that—some folks do not handle heat very well.

Everyone likes the idea of summer well enough. By early June, however, there are those of us who are completely over the stickiness, mosquitoes, and bumblebees. Left out in the sun's rays, we do not glisten like those fashionable models. No, we sweat. Thankfully, there is something akin to perfection for those who like the idea but not the reality of summer: it's the screened-in porch. With a screened-in porch, one can still interact with and be a part of summer while avoiding sunburns and bee stings.

A believer's interaction with the world is much the same way. We are not to hate the world. We are not to hide inside our air-conditioned homes and avoid all contact with anything that resembles discomfort. Sometimes we have to get out there and sweat just a little. But it's good to have some protection.

When we belong to God, the enemy does not have full access to us. Anything that comes our way is first filtered through His hands. We are not exempt from pain, but we do have the covering of the Holy Spirit, which enables us to endure. It's kind of like walking around with one's very own screened-in porch.

There are times, Lord, when I feel weary and worn. I realize in those moments that I have given a little too much of myself to the world. Remind me, Father, to stay close to Your covering so that I am protected from that which would harm me.

RAISING BABIES

Except Caleb the son of Jephunneh. He shall see it, and to
him and to his children I will give the land on which he has
trodden, because he has wholly followed the LORD!

DEUTERONOMY 1:36 ESV

Mothers are not perfect. We mess up all the time. We spend too much time tidying up messes that will reappear and not enough time enjoying moments that will never come again. Maybe we are too quick to tell our children to go play instead of asking them to come and sit. We easily get caught up in the to-do list of motherhood.

Feed the baby.
Change the diaper.
Fold the laundry.
Make the dinner.

There is one area, however, where we simply cannot allow ourselves to fail. We must be completely committed to God and faithful in our walk with Him. We'll never be perfect, but we can be faithful. Falling short in this area could cause future generations—our children and grandchildren—to suffer.

In Deuteronomy, Caleb's generation was called an evil generation. What was it that stopped this evil generation from seeing the promised land? They chose fear over faith, timidity over trust. They focused on what they could see instead of what God promised, and they paid dearly for it.

We must choose faith, and we must choose to trust the promises of God. We must choose these things for ourselves because we are desperate for God's

presence and for our children because we are desperate to see His promises
fulfilled in them.

It's easy to focus on fear, Lord. Fear is an in-my-face
kind of enemy. Help me instead to choose You.

GUARDING YOUR GARDEN

Above all else, guard your heart, for everything you do flows from it.

PROVERBS 4:23

At first, it's all fun and games as you walk through the garden center to pick out the perfect plants before lovingly placing them into the ground. Visions of fresh strawberries and tomatoes dance in your head as you parade through your garden with your brand-new watering can and post pictures on social media. It's easy to be diligent when spring breezes are blowing and everything is fresh and new.

But there comes a point when gardening is no longer the enjoyment it once was. The sun beats down, and the bees buzz. It's time for the hard work of ensuring that your garden isn't overrun by pests and devoured by critters. It's easy to become a little less enthusiastic and diligent, until one morning you awake to find that a rabbit has helped itself to all of your tomato plants. It's then you realize that you didn't properly guard your garden.

Sometimes we guard our hearts like an amateur gardener. We're diligent for a while, spending time in the Word and posting our favorite Bible verses on our social media accounts. We're quick to share the latest and greatest thing and hashtag it #blessed. Eventually, however, guarding our hearts becomes real work. The enemy attempts to distract us with shiny things. Friends don't share our convictions, and friction develops. As we are bombarded with ungodly messages and negativity, self-discipline becomes difficult. All of these things seek to draw our hearts away from God.

Our lives reflect the condition of our hearts. If our hearts aren't fed and watered daily with the Word of God and prayer, we may just awaken to find that the enemy has helped himself to the fruits of our joy and peace.

Lord, give me wisdom regarding what I do and do not allow to enter my heart. Help me to diligently maintain my relationship with You. May the fruit of my life be proof that my heart belongs to You.

EATING WATERMELON

Now these Jews were more noble than those in Thessalonica;
they received the word with all eagerness, examining the
Scriptures daily to see if these things were so.

ACTS 17:11 ESV

There's something wonderful about cutting into a cold watermelon on a hot day, with its beautiful green exterior and juicy, red flesh. It would be easy to simply inhale such a fabulous treat without a second thought. However, there's one tiny problem. Actually, many tiny problems. Watermelons have seeds.

You have to carefully examine your chunk of melon to make sure that you aren't swallowing something you shouldn't. And don't even get me started on so-called seedless watermelons. (Spoiler alert: they aren't seedless!) It doesn't matter if you believe seeds should be removed prior to chewing or if you're the type that prefers spittin'. The important thing to know is what to ingest and what to reject.

Much like a nice, ripe watermelon, a lot of biblical teaching can appear quite lovely on the surface. If it's what we want to hear, it's tempting to take it all in without a second thought. But all teaching should be examined in light of God's Word. What holds true should be ingested, and anything false should be rejected.

Even in church circles, some strive for popularity over truth. No matter who's teaching and no matter how great it sounds, we must examine it by the light of God's Word so we don't accidentally swallow a seed.

There are so many opinions and ideas presenting themselves as truth, Lord. Give me the wisdom to measure everything against Your Word and to take in only that which You say is true.

DIY

But Moses replied in the LORD's presence, "Since I am such
a poor speaker, how will Pharaoh listen to me?"

EXODUS 6:30 HCSB

It used to be that if you had a problem with your toilet, you would call a plumber. If you had some faulty lighting, an electrician was the person to call. Whatever your need may have been, the logical thing to do was to get in touch with an expert in that area. Most folks would never have considered shingling their own roofs or remodeling their own kitchens. There are professionals for that sort of thing.

Then the DIY movement took over. People began to realize that, with just a little guidance, they could do just about anything. Instead of reaching for the phone, a person can simply watch a how-to video and do it herself. A little confidence and the proper tools are all that is necessary.

Sometimes God calls people to do things that they may think would be better left to the professionals. The Bible, however, is full of DIYers. Moses didn't consider himself qualified to speak to Pharaoh, but he did. Even Paul admitted that he wasn't the most eloquent speaker, yet he preached the gospel everywhere he went. Gideon didn't feel like a warrior, but God called him to be one.

Scripture is full of ordinary men and women doing extraordinary things with just a little courage and the willingness to obey. It wasn't a seasoned mother, but a virgin girl chosen to raise the Son of God. It wasn't theologians but fishermen whom Christ called to follow Him.

Don't wait until you feel qualified to do what God is calling you to do. If He wanted a "professional," He would have chosen one! A willing and teachable

DIYer can do more for God than someone who thinks they already know everything.

I don't have to know everything, Lord. I just need to know and trust You. I offer my talents and my life to You to be used as You see fit.

BIRD'S-EYE VIEW

For the eyes of the LORD run to and fro throughout the whole earth, to
give strong support to those whose heart is blameless toward him.

2 CHRONICLES 16:9 ESV

From my perch on the deck, I have a clear view of the entire yard. The children can be seen, and their squeals of delight can be heard (and arguments over the swing can be ignored). With so many little ones, my eyes are constantly scanning the yard, back and forth, keeping tabs on each child.

The children know that their mama is on the deck and find security in knowing that I'm constantly watching them. Yet even knowing this, they occasionally call up to me.

"Mommy, did you see that?"

"Mommy, watch this!"

Though they know that, as a group, they are being watched, each individual child still needs to know that she is seen. She needs to know that her accomplishments are noted. She needs to know that, if something were to go wrong, it would not go unnoticed.

Adults are the same way. We understand that God is constantly looking over His creation, and we take security in knowing that He watches over us as a whole. Yet, sometimes we still need to know that He sees us individually—that He's applauding when we succeed and that He's aware when we're hurting.

There are times when we call out to Him.

"God, did You see that?"

"God, watch this!"

When we do, His response is much like mine: "I sure did, honey. I saw the whole thing."

Sometimes it's a breeze on my skin. Other times, it's a nudge in my heart. Thank You, Lord, for letting me know that You see me in the midst of all creation.

NOSY NEIGHBORS

You should mind your own business.

1 THESSALONIANS 4:11

My family was new in town, and we were standing in my front yard chatting with a member of the local church who lived nearby. She was telling me about some event that I had missed the night before and then ever-so-casually said, "I looked in all of your windows to see if you were home, but the blinds were all closed."

Now, I don't have anything to hide. If you peeked in my windows right now, you would likely find me wearing yoga pants and drinking coffee. In that moment, however, I was forever indebted to the inventor of window blinds.

Most of us, at one time or another, have had a nosy neighbor. If we are honest, many of us have been nosy neighbors. When we live so close to other folks, it's difficult not to wonder what may be going on behind closed doors.

Perhaps this tendency is one reason why, in a section discussing brotherly love, Paul told believers to mind their own business. Right there, in between the instructions to live quietly and to work hard, is the directive not to peek in your neighbor's windows. (That is my paraphrase, but I think Paul would agree.)

There is no question that we are to love our neighbors; Scripture is quite clear on that subject. But we need to do so without crossing boundaries. I'm thinking the front door might be a good place to start.

Lord, teach me to love my neighbors well. Help me to set a good example by concerning myself with the affairs of my own household and not meddling in the affairs of others.

INHERITANCES

The boundary lines have fallen for me in pleasant
places; surely I have a delightful inheritance.

PSALM 16:6

What kind of inheritance are you expecting? Are you hoping to get your grandmother's antique china? Perhaps you have an understanding with your siblings regarding your mama's jewelry. On the other hand, are there some items you are hoping go to someone else? Whatever your expectations may be, chances are that the items are rich in history but small in earthly value. Unlike in the movies, most of us will not have a mysterious, rich relative pass away and bestow their wealth upon us. As for me, I tease my father that he has spent my entire earthly inheritance on Harley T-shirts and motorcycle chrome.

As Christ-followers, we know that He is currently preparing a place for each of us. We aren't told what it will look like exactly. The psalmist is certain, however, that it will be delightful! There's no earthly treasure that can compare with the beauty that awaits us.

Our inheritance is Christ's very presence. When we reach heaven, we'll never again long for Him. He will forever be in our sight and by our side. The psalmist, in Psalm 16, declared that there is fullness of joy in the presence of Christ. Our inheritance is eternal joy.

The temporary happiness that we fight for on earth will not compare to the perfect joy found in His presence. His joy is more than enough; it is full and abundant. It is the perfect inheritance after a lifetime of following the Savior. One day we will stand in His presence, and whatever He has prepared will be more than enough.

Of all the treasures that heaven holds, the most precious will be Your presence, Lord. No earthly inheritance could ever compare.

DRINKING FROM THE WATER HOSE

Jesus answered her, "If you knew the gift of God and who it is that asks you for a drink, you would have asked him and he would have given you living water."

JOHN 4:10

During the summer months, my children play outside for hours each day. The freedom to imagine, climb trees, and get dirty are some of the best elements of childhood. Unfortunately, the constant in-and-out of the house and the numerous requests for water fill up those days as well.

I recently watched as one of my children came in for a drink. She filled up a little plastic cup and made her way back outside. As she walked, water splashed out with each step. By the time she reached the backyard, there was hardly any water left. Within minutes, she was thirsty again and returning for more.

Although it certainly wasn't an ideal way to quench her thirst, it was the only way she knew, so I led her back outside and over to the water spigot. She listened intently as I explained that, with a turn of the knob, she could have unlimited water. No more trips back and forth with a tiny plastic cup.

When Jesus encountered the woman at the well, she was retrieving water the only way she knew how. It was normal for women to journey to the well before the heat of the day, completing a task that had to be performed over and over again if the families were going to have water. They knew no other way.

But this woman was amazed when Jesus said there was another way. The water He offered was a never-ending source of life. While she was seeking water to satisfy physical needs, He was offering far more. Jesus was offering Himself.

There are times when I foolishly attempt to quench the thirst in my soul with a little plastic cup, when You, Lord, are the never-ending fountain. Only You can satisfy the longing in me.

S'MORES

"So, because you are lukewarm, and neither hot nor cold, I will spit you out of my mouth."

REVELATION 3:16 ESV

According to the calendar, the first day of summer is June 21. However, in my opinion, summer begins the first time you gather your loved ones around a fire and make your first s'more. Something about the crunchy crackers, gooey marshmallow, and melted chocolate screams fun and freedom. A s'more is all kinds of wonderful.

Before you consume one of these delicious treats, you need to know one thing: there's no polite way to eat a s'more—it's an all-or-nothing sort of deal. If you don't get chocolate on your chin and marshmallow all over your fingers, you haven't fully embraced the experience.

Much like eating a s'more, following Christ is all-or-nothing. Too much is at stake for believers to be concerned about appearances. Wishy-washy faith is distasteful. The Lord desires and deserves much more from His followers.

If we are to love as Christ loved, then we have to get our hands dirty. We must move beyond sanitary, random acts of kindness and into the realm of true servanthood, where things get sticky. We aren't called to a sterile existence. We are called to a messy, chocolate-on-our-faces, all-in kind of life. It may be scary at times, but we'll never look back with regret when we love people.

I don't ever want to be lukewarm when it comes to You, Lord. Help me to choose the messiness that often comes with loving people over the seemingly sanitary but selfish life.

TRASH DAY

If we confess our sins, he is faithful and just and will forgive
us our sins and purify us from all unrighteousness.

1 JOHN 1:9

Trash day is a funny thing. You certainly want it to come, but you likely dread the whole trash removal process—emptying the various household trash cans and attempting to make it all fit in the large outside receptacle that always seems to smell like death. A certain finesse is necessary to roll it to the curb while touching it as little as possible because, again, it's a bunch of trash.

We may even feel a certain amount of embarrassment in rolling the trash to the end of the drive. Some do it late in the evening or early in the morning, hoping they won't be seen. Why is that? Everyone has trash. What's the big deal?

The removal of trash from our homes is much like the confession of sins, and we're often embarrassed by the sheer amount of it. Most of us cannot stand the smell of our own trash and can only assume that others would be completely grossed out by it too. However, if we were honest with one another, we would find that our trash is an awful lot alike. It's more than one person can deal with alone. We could all use some help rolling our cans to the curb.

Like trash, sin needs to be dealt with on an ongoing basis. Letting it pile up and then desperately trying to remove it from our lives before the garbage truck pulls up is too overwhelming. Each day, we must examine our hearts to determine what needs to be discarded. After all, everyone has trash that needs to be dealt with, but nobody has to do it alone.

I am so grateful, Lord, that You don't turn away
from me because of my sin. Thank You for being
a forgiving God who is faithful and just.

THE ICE CREAM TRUCK

He satisfies the longing soul.

PSALM 107:9 NKJV

Few things thrill the soul more than the sound of an ice cream truck on a hot summer day. In neighborhoods everywhere, children wait anxiously on their front steps for the truck to finally turn down their street. At the sight of the brightly decorated truck, they rush up with their quarters.

Once at the truck, each child has his or her choice of frozen treats: ice cream sandwiches, shaved ice, rainbow pops, or orange sherbet push-ups. However, occasionally, there's the heartache of gathering one's money and hurrying to the truck, only to discover that there are no more orange sherbet push-ups. In those moments, a sad life lesson is learned: sometimes the ice cream truck delivers only disappointment.

All of humanity walks around with a longing soul. We long for meaning and purpose, to be known and loved. The world will play a pretty tune to get our attention and then present us with some seemingly good treats. A little praise of man here and a little financial success there, and for a moment, it feels nice.

The treats that the world offers, however, are only temporary pleasures that melt under the hot sun of life. They satisfy for a season but fail to provide any long-term solution to the longing of the soul. We'll never know true satisfaction until we encounter Christ. Once we know Him, nothing the world offers will do—not even if it is covered in chocolate and sprinkled with nuts.

I long to be satisfied, Lord. Help me to remember that true satisfaction is found only in You. Everything else the world offers is a poor substitute.

FAMILY RESEMBLANCE

Then God said, "Let us make man in our image, after our likeness."

GENESIS 1:26 ESV

Who in your family do you resemble the most? Do you have your mom's nose, your dad's hairline, or your grandmother's eyes? Folks take a lot of pride in family resemblances. If you have biological children, you probably beam with pride every time someone says that your child looks like you. Certain characteristics carry on throughout many generations.

The beginning of Genesis gives us a peek into the masterpiece that was God's original creation. Blue skies and sparkling water were put into place with a word. Yet, after days of creating, there was one thing God still desired to create. God wanted something that would look like Him.

He could have made man in any form or fashion. He chose, however, for us to resemble Him. God wanted to watch us as a proud Father and be able to say, *I see Myself in her.* And when others look at us, they should see some of Him too. When we go out of our way to help the hurting, we resemble Him. When we put the needs of others ahead of our own, we are bearing His image.

Our God is a very creative God. He created us all individually with unique gifts and talents. We each have a plan for our lives outlined by the One who created us. But sometimes we get caught up in our own image. We want to showcase our gifts. We want to be seen and make it all about us.

When God created Adam, He didn't list his spiritual strengths. He didn't outline the entire plan for Adam's life. No, God looked at His ultimate creation and said, *This one here will resemble Me.* It was always His intention that there be a family resemblance.

I long to look like You, Lord. Mold me into
Your image so that when others look my way,
they see that I look like my Father.

A SHADY PLACE TO SIT

It will be a shelter and shade from the heat of the day.

ISAIAH 4:6

There are two types of people. The first are those who bake themselves in the sun and somehow enjoy it. Sweat seems to bring them joy. The stifling air doesn't seem to bother them. Their ability to withstand the heat is baffling.

Then there are the rest of us. We are the ones who check the temperature and the humidity before ever stepping foot outside, sunscreen and sunglasses in hand. We can endure a summer day as long as we have a glass of iced tea in hand and a shady place to sit. Because, let's face it, shade makes the sun bearable.

When Isaiah described what life would be like for God's people when the Messiah appeared, he used the imagery of shade during the heat of the day. When summer is at its hottest, and you think you can't last another moment in the sun, it's amazing what a little time in the shade will do. Without changing anything in terms of the sun's heat or brightness, a little shade enables a person to endure the heat for just a little bit longer.

Jesus is shade on a hot summer day for believers. When life seems to be overwhelming or unbearable, a little time with Jesus can give us the needed strength to make it through the day. Though our circumstances may not change, His presence brings relief from the heat of the moment. When we sit in His shade, we are refreshed before heading back out into the heat of the day.

Without You, Lord, this life would be unbearable. The heat of the day would be too much. Thank You for being my shade and my place of refreshment.

LEMONADE STAND

He opened the rock, and water gushed out; it flowed like a river in the desert.

PSALM 105:41

At a certain point in the middle of summer, you'll likely feel as though you cannot survive another moment of heat. You break a sweat walking to the mailbox. You know exactly how much of your body you can squeeze into the freezer. You give up watering the lawn, and instead you sit in a chair and water yourself. Not to be overly dramatic, but you're pretty sure you're going to die.

When you've reached this point, nothing brings more joy than to see the little girl next door set up a lemonade stand. You blink a couple of times to make sure the heat isn't causing hallucinations. Then, moving slowly, using as little energy as possible, you leave the safety of your oscillating fan for a paper cup of lemonade-flavored heaven. And you realize that you will, in fact, live to sweat another day.

On their journey through the desert, there were many times when the children of Israel thought that they couldn't make it another moment. It didn't matter what miracles God had performed previously; they were certain they were going to die. We know the end of the story, so we're quick to judge. But how often have we done the same thing?

Maybe we receive an unexpected bill and panic because we can't see any way of paying it. Someone we love is ill, and we are devastated because we cannot fix them. We fall into that same old pit of sin that we've climbed out of multiple times and wonder if God can forgive us. And we forget how God has repeatedly provided, healed, and forgiven in the past. In the midst of a current crisis, we forget all He has done before. We forget that God can send water gushing from a rock in the middle of the desert.

When the heat of your circumstances seems to be too much, don't panic. When you feel parched and dry, don't think you're beyond help. Look around. God may have just set up a lemonade stand in the middle of your hot summer afternoon.

Too often, Lord, I'm tempted to panic. I focus on my circumstances and forget that, with You, nothing is impossible. Thank You for the tender care You show even in the face of my doubt.

PLAY DOUGH

As has just been said: "Today, if you hear his voice, do not harden your hearts as you did in the rebellion."

Most parents have a love-hate relationship with play dough. Sure, it entertains the children. Yes, it encourages them to use their imaginations. Play dough is a fairly inexpensive way to ward off boredom on a rainy day. The play dough experience has its benefits.

It only takes one use, however, to understand the not-so-pleasant side of play dough. One innocent afternoon of children being creative can result in little bits of colored dough being found all over the house for days to come. It'll be stuck to tables, mashed into carpet, and hidden in toy boxes. Play dough has a way of invading the house.

Yet, the play dough invasion is not the most frustrating part. If not put away properly each and every time, play dough becomes hard. And there is nothing fun about hard play dough. Nothing pretty or useful can be molded from it. It cracks at the first attempt to bend it. The only thing that can be done with hardened play dough is to toss it.

Our hearts need to be like a freshly opened container of play dough in the hands of God. We must be soft and pliable. When we allow ourselves to be molded according to His will, He can make something lovely and useful out of our lives. There's no limit to what He can do with us.

Disobedience and rebellion, however, will harden a believer's heart. When we fail to obey God's will or to spend time in prayer and Bible study, we become as useless as dried-up play dough.

I long to be used by You, Lord. Mold me into Your image and bend my heart toward Your will. Forgive me for the times when I have hardened my heart.

HUMMINGBIRD VINES

A little yeast works through the whole batch of dough.

GALATIANS 5:9

Some plants serve double duty when planted in a yard. Lavender, for example, is said to repel mosquitoes. Marigolds, when mixed in with vegetable gardens, keep away unwanted pests. Then there's the hummingbird vine. If you have an area that you'd like to cover, either for visual appeal or privacy, the hummingbird vine is the way to go. Just know, however, that with very little effort on your part, that small starter plant will grow and grow and grow. Sometimes something very small can grow out of control.

Paul warned against this kind of thing in Galatians. What may seem small and insignificant, when left unchecked, can work its way through a person's life. A little hummingbird vine can overtake a whole porch. A little yeast can make its way through a whole batch of dough. And a little bit of sin can affect an entire life. So we must be diligent in examining ourselves and the world around us.

It's natural to want to classify sin. Often we look at something in our own lives and consider it a minor infraction; however, the sin we see in someone else's life may seem like a doozy. The truth is, there are no degrees of sin. There is just sin. And any sin that isn't handled properly will eventually work its way into every aspect of our lives—much like the hummingbird vine but without the beauty. It doesn't matter if you plant the tangerine beauty or the yellow trumpet creeper, if you give it its way, the hummingbird vine will completely take over. And so will sin.

Sometimes, I want to see my sin as less serious than it truly is, Lord. Help me to see the true nature behind the things I allow into my life. Teach me to daily examine my heart to ensure that nothing is growing unchecked.

CAST IRON SKILLET

I am reminded of your sincere faith, a faith that dwelt first in your grandmother
Lois and your mother Eunice and now, I am sure, dwells in you as well.

2 TIMOTHY 1:5 ESV

Certain treasured items get passed down from one generation to the next. Old photographs, newspaper clippings, and military medals become precious keepsakes after loved ones are gone. In my family, the hand-me-down of all hand-me-downs, however, is Mawmaw's cast iron skillet.

Cast iron is the star of any country kitchen, generously seasoned with love and lard. It's created to withstand high temperatures and must never be submerged in water. If treated properly, cast iron is virtually indestructible. Multiple generations have eaten cornbread out of Mawmaw's skillet, and everyone secretly hopes it will one day be in his or her cabinet.

Even better than Mawmaw's cast iron, however, is a sincere faith that is handed down through the years. Several times in Scripture, believers are instructed to pass on their faith to future generations. We are to tell our children the wonders that the Lord has wrought in our lives and to be an example of patience and perseverance.

God promises to show His love to a thousand generations of those who love Him and are obedient to His Word (Exodus 20:6). When we are faithful Christ-followers, our children, grandchildren, and future generations will inherit the blessings of our faithfulness. That's a legacy worth leaving.

It's okay if you don't have that family legacy in your past; it can begin with you. You can be the one to develop a deep, abiding faith that is passed down for generations to come.

I long to pass on a legacy of faith to my children and grandchildren, Lord. When I'm long gone, I want them to know that I was a woman who was desperate for You.

HOMESICK

*He who testifies to these things says, "Yes, I am
coming soon." Amen. Come, Lord Jesus.*

REVELATION 22:20

What is it that reminds you of home? Is it a long gravel driveway, the smell of honeysuckle in the air, or a weathered front porch? Whether it's a sight, a sound, or a smell, everyone has something that means home to them. For many of us, it's a person who makes us long for home. The profile of a stranger in the store reminds you of Grandma, and in an instant you're transported back to your childhood home. An old photograph falls out of your Bible, and you're reminded of a friend from long ago. And before you know it, you're homesick.

John was intimately acquainted with Jesus during His earthly ministry. On more than one occasion, John referred to himself as the beloved disciple. Jesus loved John, and the feeling was certainly mutual. With that in mind, imagine what John surely felt when he was given a vision from Christ about future events. The memories must have flooded back when John saw "one like a son of man" (Revelation 14:14). How homesick John must have been for his Savior.

In Ecclesiastes 3:11, it says that God has put eternity in our hearts. Something in us longs for a home that we have never seen. Scripture gives us glimpses of it, and we long to be there. Somehow we know. We look around, and we know that this world isn't home. We get a little homesick.

But it won't be long. Jesus has promised that He is preparing a place for us. I don't know what it looks like, but I know that it will feel like home.

Lord, I get so homesick. This world can be an unfriendly place, and I long to rest in Your presence. I want to see, with my eyes, the eternity that You placed in my heart long ago.

HOWDY, NEIGHBOR!

"I have called you by name, you are mine."

ISAIAH 43:1 ESV

Have you ever been sitting on your porch or working in your yard and had a neighbor greet you by name? It's a good feeling. When someone remembers your name, it's as if they're saying that you're worth remembering (which, by the way, you are). A friendly wave is great, but when it's accompanied by a personal greeting, a person just can't help but smile.

Sometimes people know who you are based on your relationship to others. Perhaps you are so-and-so's sister. Or maybe you are the pastor's wife or the mom with the twins. When folks remember something specific about you, especially if it is something you take pride in, it also feels good.

Something deep within us desires to be seen and remembered. We long to be seen as worth remembering. It is, therefore, no small thing when someone calls us by our name.

In Isaiah 43, we learn that, because of their disobedience, the Israelites were plundered and imprisoned. For a time, they had forgotten who they were. God, however, did not forget. He remembered exactly who they were and to whom they belonged. The God who created them knew them by name and, even in the face of their disobedience, reminded them of their connection to Him. "You are mine," He told them.

There's no way around it. We will encounter seasons of difficulty in life. Whether through our own disobedience or because of things beyond our control, the storms of life will rage. In those moments, the enemy would love for us to forget who we are and to believe that God has forgotten us as well.

God, however, doesn't forget. Even in the midst of their shame, He reminded the Israelites of their connection to Him. When we stumble, He reminds us of that same connection. He knows our name. We belong to Him.

Thank You, Lord, for Your faithfulness to Your children. When I forget who I am, I can look to Your Word and be reminded, time after time, that I belong to You.

AN HONEST FRIEND

Faithful are the wounds of a friend.

PROVERBS 27:6 ESV

As a friend, there are certain times when you hold your tongue. For instance, you don't tell an exhausted new mom that she looks like she's been hit by a Mack truck. Instead, you tell her she looks fabulous. She'll know you're being gracious, and she'll love you for it. Or when you show up and she has painted her entire living room the worst shade of green you have ever seen, you applaud her efforts and change the subject.

However, there are those times when your friend is counting on you to tell her the truth. She needs to know, prior to presenting her speech to the entire PTA, that she has lipstick on her teeth. She needs to know that you won't let her make a grand entrance to a party with toilet paper stuck to her shoe. She needs to know that, if needed, you'll pull her aside and let her know that a pair of her daughter's underwear is stuck to the back of her sweater. (These things really happen, y'all!)

Real friends are honest friends. While flattery feels good for a moment, a truth-telling friend can be trusted for a lifetime. Sometimes this means that a friend will tell you something you don't want to hear. We all need a Christ-following friend who is not afraid to tell us when we're straying into dangerous territory. Yes, feelings may be hurt when she points out our negative attitude or tendency to judge, but we can trust that her words are for our own good.

With social media, people too often feel the freedom to criticize or judge others they barely know. But the fact is that it takes time and face-to-face conversations to earn the right to speak into someone's life. When someone has loved us, cried with us, and rejoiced with us, we can trust her words even when they hurt.

Give me the grace, Lord, to accept the faithful wounds of a friend. Grant me the love and boldness to be a truth-speaking friend when needed.

STARGAZING

The heavens declare the glory of God, and the
sky above proclaims his handiwork.

PSALM 19:1 ESV

If you only study your immediate surroundings, it may seem that you're in control of your life. You pay your bills and care for your family. You maintain the lawn and protect your home. If something needs to be done, you do it. If something is broken, you fix it. So when sitting on your front porch on a random Tuesday afternoon, you may feel like the ruler of your little corner of the world.

Or perhaps when you look around, you feel as though you aren't in control at all. Your world may seem to be spinning out of control because of illness, job loss, or family drama. It could be that fear and anxiety have crept in until you've completely lost perspective. You may sit on your front porch on a random Tuesday afternoon and wonder who is in control of your little corner of the world.

If you sit on that same porch late at night, however, the truth is revealed. When the distractions and noise of the day are done and the silent night settles in, you have a chance to be still. Just a few minutes of studying the night sky will make you realize how very small you are in the grand scheme of things and that you are not in control. None of us is. Perhaps, at first, that's scary or overwhelming. But if you gaze a little longer, the hand of the Creator becomes evident. The glory of God is declared through the shining of the stars.

So, whether you're feeling overly confident or a little insecure about your place in the world, take a look at the night sky. Stargazing will remind you that the God who created the world is in control of it, and He loves you.

Lord, I fluctuate between arrogance and insecurity when it comes to my place in the world. Thank You for the night sky and its reminder that I can trust my corner of the world to the One who created it.

A SHRIMP BOIL

His disciples asked him what this parable meant.

LUKE 8:9 NLT

Early into our relationship, my soon-to-be husband invited me to a family get-together. It was going to be at the beach, and I was assured that I was in for a real treat come dinnertime. My beloved asked me if I liked to eat boiled shrimp, and because I was afraid of looking foolish, I assured him that I loved it.

It might be important to note that my man comes from a long line of Louisiana Cajuns. My people, on the other hand, are from Ohio, where we get our shrimp at Red Lobster, and it comes breaded with a loaded baked potato on the side.

As we arrived for the meal later that evening, we were greeted by the smell of seafood. As the guest, I was ushered to the front of the line. I made my way into the kitchen, and that's when I saw them. Dozens of shrimp were piled in the sink, and unlike the popcorn shrimp from Red Lobster, these had eyes.

Sometimes a person needs a little clarification. In Luke 8, Jesus told a parable about a sower and some seeds, soil, and thorns. The disciples just couldn't make sense of it. So, instead of assuming they knew the meaning or pretending to understand, they asked Him to clarify. Jesus then explained, in great detail, what He meant by each part of the parable.

God doesn't expect us to understand everything. His ways are far higher than ours. It's okay to admit that we don't understand something or to ask for more details. It is okay to ask, "What do you mean by *boiled shrimp*?" Otherwise, you may find yourself looking at a dinner that's looking back at you.

Lord, sometimes I want to appear as if I understand everything. Teach me to admit when I'm just not sure. You are a patient God and the granter of wisdom to those who ask for it.

REPURPOSING

Therefore, if anyone is in Christ, he is a new creation. The
old has passed away; behold, the new has come.

2 CORINTHIANS 5:17 ESV

Repurposing old furniture is quite the rage these days. People will dig through dumpsters and spend their Saturdays scouring yard sales hoping for a trash-to-treasure find. Anything old can be made new again. An old desk becomes a baby's changing table. An antique bureau is transformed into a bathroom vanity. An infant's crib can now be a child's art station. The things a person can do with an old wooden pallet will blow your mind! Thanks to the Internet and television shows, people are learning that something doesn't have to be what it has always been.

For some, however, it's difficult to catch the vision. It's hard to look at an old wooden door and envision that it could become a dinner table. A person can get stuck on what something used to be and struggle to see its potential. While this may be the latest-and-greatest fad in home design, Scripture is full of transformation stories. God was repurposing before repurposing was cool.

God took Saul, called him Paul, and transformed a murderer into a missionary. Though he looked the same and some struggled to view him differently, God had given Paul a new passion and a new purpose.

God found Gideon hiding in fear. Gideon saw himself as weak, but God looked at him and saw that he could be a warrior.

A woman interrupted a dinner party full of people who only saw her sin, but Jesus saw her potential to be more. She walked in as "that woman," and she walked out knowing love and forgiveness.

God has always been about the business of transforming people into His image. Because of Christ, anyone can be made new and given a new purpose in life. No one has to be resigned to simply being what they've always been. It's possible to be repurposed.

Thank You, Lord, for loving me enough to make me new. The old has passed away, and I don't have to be what I have been.

LIGHTNING BUGS

The eyes of the Lord are in every place.

PROVERBS 15:3 ESV

Summer evenings can be incredibly peaceful. The heat of the day is done. The kids are bathed and calm. The neighborhood is settled, and the world is dark. It was just such a night when one of my daughters came outside to sit with me. The stars were hidden on this overcast evening, making it darker than usual, and my daughter was afraid.

Then we saw it. One little lightning bug flew near us and briefly lit up. As our eyes adjusted to the darkness, we began to see more lightning bugs. Suddenly, the yard seemed to be filled with little specks of light. My daughter turned to me and said, "If it hadn't been so dark, we might have missed them."

In His Word, Jesus promised that we would experience trials and hardships. Life holds seasons of darkness, and darkness can be scary. For the Christ-follower, however, it's never a complete darkness. Again and again in Scripture, God has promised to never leave us. We don't need to be afraid or try to hide. We just need to pause and give our eyes a chance to adjust, seeking those little specks of light. We can be confident that they are there because He has promised that He is there.

Once we stop focusing on the dark, we'll begin to see glimmers of light everywhere. We will see Him and know Him in a way that we might have missed if it had not been so dark.

The darkness would be a scary place, Lord, if You were not in it. When I'm tempted to focus on the dark, help me to see the light instead.

A SCREEN DOOR

Show hospitality to one another without grumbling.

1 PETER 4:9 ESV

Gertie lived during a time when folks dropped by without notice and were welcomed without hesitation. Her screen door opened and closed multiple times a day. The spring was long broken, causing the door to bang loudly against the door frame. As the sound echoed throughout the house, a friend or relative would walk into the kitchen.

Gertie was never annoyed or put out by an unexpected visitor. No one took off his or her shoes at the door or apologized for showing up unannounced. Unscheduled visits were always welcome, and there was always a pot of coffee and an empty chair in Gertie's kitchen.

Jesus' ministry relied heavily on the hospitality of the early church. On more than one occasion, He relaxed and had a meal in the home of Martha, Mary, and Lazarus. Without any warning at all, He instructed Zacchaeus to get out of the tree because He was staying at his home that very day. Scripture says that Zacchaeus "came down at once and welcomed him gladly" (Luke 19:6).

The command regarding hospitality is that it is done without grumbling. In Romans 12:13, Paul listed hospitality among the characteristics of a Christian. Along with loving one another and being patient in affliction is the instruction to "seek to show hospitality" (ESV). Hospitality isn't only a response to unexpected visitors; we are to seek out opportunities to demonstrate it.

We live in a world of solid front doors and deadbolts, where most people feel uncomfortable showing up unannounced. Even coffee dates among friends are planned days or weeks in advance. Hospitality, however, welcomes the unexpected creak of a screen door.

Lord, help me to seek to show others hospitality. Open my eyes to opportunities to receive and serve those around me. May I gladly greet unexpected guests with an empty chair and a listening ear.

COMING HOME

Behold, He is coming with clouds.

REVELATION 1:7 NKJV

For much of my childhood, my dad was a truck driver. I have lots of memories of truck-stop diners and jukebox music. I know all of the lingo and the words to every Willie Nelson song. Watching my dad's truck disappear into the distance with one last blow of the air horn, I would begin counting the days until he came home.

As the time approached for him to return, I would wait impatiently on the front porch. I knew which direction he would come from and that I would hear him before I saw him. So, I watched and waited, not wanting to miss his truck as it rounded the corner. I wanted to be the first to see him and let him know I had been expecting him.

In the second chapter of the gospel of Luke, there's a story about a man named Simeon. He had been promised by the Holy Spirit that he would not see death until he had seen the Christ. Every day when he awoke, he knew that it could be the day. He waited with the expectation of seeing Christ.

As Christ-followers, we should be living with the same anticipation surrounding His return. Scripture tells us that His appearance could be at any moment. We should be watching and waiting, with the understanding as we wake each day that this could be the day Jesus returns to take us home. When Christ returns, we should be able to say, "Ah, I have been expecting You."

Lord, teach me to live in expectation of Your return, and instill in me a sense of urgency for those who do not know You.

CLOTHES ON A LINE

Bear one another's burdens, and so fulfill the law of Christ.

GALATIANS 6:2 NKJV

You may remember the days when folks washed their dirty clothes in a washtub in the yard and then hung them on a clothesline to dry. Nowadays most would shudder at the idea of people driving by and seeing their unmentionables blowing in the breeze. You might imagine the neighbors talking among themselves and wondering if you even own a pair of matching socks.

But thankfully someone invented a machine that allowed people to keep all of their dirty laundry behind closed doors. Indoor laundry is convenient and private. No one has to know that your bath towels are falling apart or that you own more than a dozen pairs of pajama pants. People only see what you want them to see.

Unfortunately, this concealing mentality has seeped into other areas of our lives. Somewhere along the way, we became uncomfortable with other people's dirty laundry—and we certainly aren't eager to air our own. Too many of us sit in church wearing our Sunday morning happy faces, ashamed of our messes. Though we may pretend to be fine, in reality, we each have our own pain, shame, or struggle.

Christ never intended for people to bear their own burdens. Life wasn't meant to be lived that way. Pain multiplies in private. Shame flourishes in isolation. Christ came to set captives free, and no one is held more captive than the person pretending to be fine.

Maybe it's time to be more open about our struggles. A lost world is watching, and no one can relate to folks who pretend not to have any dirty laundry.

Lord, forgive me for the times I have pretended to have it all together. Help me to pursue authenticity instead of perfection and to realize that we, as Your people, cannot bear one another's burdens until we acknowledge and reveal our own dirty laundry to others.

A GLASS OF MILK

All Scripture is God–breathed and is useful for teaching,
rebuking, correcting and training in righteousness.

2 TIMOTHY 3:16

Depending on where they grew up, everyone has a home remedy for physical ailments. Grandma may have insisted that gargling with warm salt water was a cure for whatever ailed you. Some believe that drinking a little apple cider vinegar each day will extend your life. Perhaps your people place all their hopes on a cup of herbal tea.

According to my mother, all you ever really need is a nice, cold glass of milk. Does your head hurt? Have a glass of milk. Do you have indigestion? A nice glass of milk will fix you right up. Are you struggling with insomnia, menstrual cramps, or athlete's foot? Relief is as close as the nearest glass of milk. You might guess that I've had a lot of milk in my day.

We want a cure-all. We want a one-size-fits-all antidote to whatever is bothering us. And there *is* something that can address any issue we might have, but we won't find it in the pantry or refrigerator. It's God's Word, and it has something to say about every need or concern in our lives.

Is there a situation requiring some discipline? Scripture will tell you how to handle it. Do you want to grow in righteousness, grace, or some other area? Go to God's Word, and seek the truth that addresses your need. It's in there. All Scripture is God-breathed and is useful for every area of your life. It will fix whatever ails you.

We look to the world, Lord, for cure-alls and quick fixes. Teach me, instead, to turn to Your Word for answers to the questions in my life.

HOLDING HANDS

*Neither height nor depth, nor anything else in all creation, will be able
to separate us from the love of God that is in Christ Jesus our Lord.*

ROMANS 8:39

I love to watch my husband and toddler walk hand-in-hand across the yard.
It's easy strolling until they make their way to the driveway, where he
instructs her to hold tightly to his hand. And she does, holding on as tightly as
a two-year-old can hold. If she trips over a rock or loses her footing and begins
to go down, I know that if it weren't for that key element of holding hands, she
would hit the ground. But her daddy also holds on, and daddies hold on a lot
tighter than two-year-olds.

This is a beautiful picture of what it's like to walk with God. There are
times when it feels like a lovely stroll through the front yard. We're surrounded
by family and friends. Times are good, and all is well as we hold on to Him and
He holds on to us.

Then the times of difficulty come. The ground becomes uneven, and our
steps aren't as sure. Rocks cause us to stumble. Someone we love becomes ill.
A spouse leaves. A job is lost. And even though we may have been holding on as
tightly as we could, we would hit the ground for sure if God weren't also holding on to us.

This is the promise we have in Christ: nothing can separate us from the
love of God. His grip is strong, and nothing that this life throws our way can
ever make Him let go.

*I am so thankful, Lord, that nothing can ever separate me from
You. You promise that, no matter what life brings, You'll never let
go of me. I may stumble, but Your grip will always catch me.*

ROSEBUSHES

For it has been granted to you on behalf of Christ not only
to believe in him, but also to suffer for him.

PHILIPPIANS 1:29

Rosebushes add a touch of elegance and beauty to any home's landscaping. If you've ever tried to plant one, though, you know all that loveliness comes at a cost. Rosebushes need constant attention, and insects seem to adore them. But that's not the worst part. When you decide to put one of those beauties in your front yard, you'll likely feel the pain of the thorns.

Given an option, most people would choose beauty without pain. But trials, pain, and loss are to be expected in this world. We hear a sermon on grace in the midst of suffering, and we leave the church building praying that it never happens to us. Our ultimate desire is to make it through this life as unscathed as possible. We want the beauty of the rose without the pain of the thorn. But what if the real beauty of the rose is the combination of bloom and thorn?

When Paul wrote his letter to the Philippians, he referred to suffering as something being granted or given to them. He wanted them to understand that to suffer for Christ was as much a gift as believing in Him. Our goal as Christ-followers is to resemble Him. Do we ever resemble Him more than when we feel the weight of the cross on our backs? Could it be that the beauty of the Christian life is the combination of believing and suffering—the rose and the thorn?

No one desires suffering, Lord, but it's part of living in this world. My prayer is that when it's my turn, I would seek the beauty in the midst of the thorns.

OLD PHOTOGRAPHS

I will remember the deeds of the LORD; yes,
I will remember your wonders of old.

PSALM 77:11 ESV

If you're like me, you probably have an unspoken understanding with your siblings when it comes to old photographs. No one ever needs to see that picture of you with the bad perm, and no one ever needs to know that your brother loved to rock a stonewashed jean jacket back in the day.

Nothing makes a person cringe more than when the old photo album is hauled out in front of company. In that seemingly innocent stack of pages is photographic evidence of every fashion faux pas you've ever made. Each picture is covered in a plastic sleeve so that your adolescent awkwardness can be preserved for the enjoyment of future generations. There are some things that you'd just rather forget.

Over and over in Scripture, however, we are told to remember. The Lord wants us to periodically review the past and recall all His deeds. The Israelites were instructed on several occasions to remember the struggles that the Lord had brought them through and to tell those stories to future generations. It wasn't just the good stuff that they were remembering, either. In order to tell of the Lord's goodness, they had to recall their own failings as well.

The fact is that we must remember the good with the bad. Together they make up the story of God's grace in our lives. It can be tempting to tell only the stuff that we're proud of or to show only the pictures of us at our best. But that wouldn't be an accurate portrayal of our faith journey, and it would discourage those walking the same road. By sharing the good with the bad, we allow others to witness the power of God's grace in our lives.

Lord, help me to be honest about my faith journey. Make me brave enough to share my story and bold enough to share Your grace with those who need to hear both.

SHADE TREES

One of the young men answered, "Behold, I have seen a son of Jesse the Bethlehemite, who is skillful in playing, a man of valor."

1 SAMUEL 16:18 ESV

Depending on your skill or interest in gardening, you may prefer any number of things in terms of landscaping. You may want your front yard to be as maintenance-free as possible—no pruning bushes or pulling weeds for you. Or perhaps you enjoy an extravagant array of plants and truly delight in the work involved. Either way, one essential for any yard is a good shade tree.

The perfect shade tree is old and solid. It needs to be strong enough to hold tire swings and climbing kids and have lots of leaves to shield you from the heat of the day. This mixture of greatness and grace creates the perfect shade tree.

Scripture describes David in much the same way: a mixture of greatness and grace. He was known for his giftedness at playing the harp, an instrument that required gentleness. Yet, he was also known as a man of war, which required strength and courage. It was the combination of these attributes that made David the man after God's own heart. He was created to be a warrior and a musician.

As believers, we are to live a similar life. There are times when it is necessary to be bold and speak truth, and there are times when we are to be gentle and extend grace. It's vital that we seek God's will to know the proper response for each situation. When those around us are weary and worn, we can be a source of shelter and shade.

You created us to be multifaceted people. Lord, help me to know when others need my strength and when they need my shade. May I be a person of gentleness and boldness, and may I know the appropriate time for each.

PORCH SITTING

Not neglecting to meet together, as is the habit of some, but encouraging
one another, and all the more as you see the Day drawing near.

HEBREWS 10:25 ESV

It is not uncommon to go days or weeks without seeing your neighbors. You can go straight from your home, to your car in the garage, to the store, back into your garage, and back into your house without ever seeing them. You can receive and pay your bills online, eliminating the need to walk to the mailbox. Even groceries can be delivered right to your door!

In years past, when central air was a luxury, folks would sit on their porches to enjoy a cool breeze, and they could see the neighbors doing the same next door. Now all one has to do is adjust the thermostat to the desired temperature—no porch sitting required. All these modern-day conveniences make it easy to become isolated without even realizing it.

All throughout Scripture, we can find examples of believers gathering together. Worship, teaching, and meals were often enjoyed in community. In fact, the author of Hebrews warns against isolation. The believers were instructed not to neglect fellowship with other believers, for in the gathering together, there is mutual encouragement.

Loneliness can make life seem overwhelming. The longer you neglect community, the harder it becomes to connect with others. The enemy would love for you to feel stuck in your solitude. If you've been neglecting relationships with others, take a small step toward community. Open your front door, step outside, and sit on your porch. It'll be good for you.

Lord, You created us to be in community. It was never Your intention that any of us should do life alone. Remind me of the importance of opening my front door and interacting with the people You've placed in my path.

SWEET POTATO CASSEROLE

Jesus answered, "I am the way and the truth and the life.
No one comes to the Father except through me."

JOHN 14:6

There are two schools of thought when it comes to making sweet potato casserole: the crunchy pecan and brown sugar topping or the gooey marshmallow topping. You might think it doesn't really matter, but you'd be wrong. People in the South take their sweet potato casserole very seriously. But we can all agree on one thing: one doesn't make sweet potato casserole with yams from a can.

Miss Sue is the oldest lady in a little church in south Alabama. She has a lot to say about a lot of things, and one of those things is sweet potato casserole. There's only one way to make it, according to Miss Sue, and it involves work. The sweet potatoes must be chosen carefully, peeled, cooked, and mashed. There are no shortcuts or cans involved. "Why," Miss Sue would ask, "do people think there's an easier way?"

Isn't that the way with so many things? We want an easier way. We want the reward without the work. Many individuals claim to have found God in their own way. The problem is that there is no other way except Jesus. No spiritual enlightenment or good living is enough. We cannot take shortcuts. The only way to God is in the footsteps of Jesus, the way of the cross. It's a way of sacrifice. The path is narrow, and few will choose it.

In the words of Miss Sue, "You can do it another way, but in the end what you end up with is not sweet potato casserole."

Lord, I know that the life we are called to live is one of sacrifice. To be like Christ is to serve and to suffer. Give me the strength to live the servant's life.

AUTUMN LEAVES

Precious in the sight of the LORD is the death of his saints.

PSALM 116:15 ESV

For as long as I can remember, my family has taken a drive every fall to look at the leaves. There's not much that exceeds the beauty of the mountains in late October. One year my mama was planning just such a trip when my brother felt the need to cheekily offer up an observation: "You know all of those leaves are dying, right? You're driving around looking at dying leaves."

He was, of course, correct. The oranges, yellows, and reds are all beautiful indications that the leaves are, in fact, dying. As the heat of summer fades and the autumn winds begin to blow, the once-green leaves begin to change color and loosen their grip. Death is on display, both sad and lovely, all at the same time.

The death of a saint is much the same way. The body grows weak, the light in the eyes begins to dim, and movements become slower. The ending of a life is in many ways sad. Yet, when the Lord looks upon the death of one of His beloved, He sees it as "precious." The Greek word used in Psalm 116:15 is *yaqar*, which means valuable, prized, weighty, rare, splendid, and precious (Strong's Concordance #3368). It's a word as rich in meaning as the autumn leaves are in color.

When God sees one of His children nearing the end of his or her earthly life, He sees a life that mattered. No matter how many days were lived, it's a life that had weight in the world. For a Christ-follower, death is both a leaving and a coming home again. It is sad and lovely all at the same time.

I am in awe of You, Lord. You hold the power of life and death in Your hands and have made it all a thing of beauty.

BACK ROADS

When Pharaoh finally let the people go, God did not lead them
along the main road that runs through Philistine territory, even
though that was the shortest route to the Promised Land.

EXODUS 13:17 NLT

In this world, there are interstate people and there are back-roads people. I still remember the first time we took the Natchez Trace Parkway for our annual trip to Granny's house. I was miserable.

Truth be told, I've always been more of an interstate kind of girl. When I was young, my dad would plan road trips carefully. Every gas stop and bathroom break was mapped out in advance. Vacation began when you arrived at your destination. The drives there and back were just necessary evils.

So, to me, Natchez Trace was *slow*. It was long stretches of nothing but us, the open road, and occasionally another traveler whom I could only assume was as wretchedly unhappy as I was. The last couple of years, however, the parkway has grown on me. I've come to the realization that life wasn't meant to be lived quickly.

It's easy to get caught up in getting from point A to point B. Maybe point B, for you, is naptime or payday. You're not interested in the potential lessons or beauty in the moment; you just want to get to where you're going and be done with it. I get it. However, there are some things we can only see and some blessings we can only receive on the slow road. If we'll take a deep breath and choose to be in the moment, we'll find ourselves seeing and experiencing things that we never would have noticed from the interstate.

Your ways are higher than my ways, Lord. Sometimes I don't understand the roads that You make me travel. Teach me to trust You as You guide me down the appropriate paths.

CLEANING THE MICROWAVE

*"The Lord does not look at the things people look at. People look
at the outward appearance, but the Lord looks at the heart."*

1 SAMUEL 16:7

There are probably certain parts of your home that you always clean before guests arrive. You may run the vacuum cleaner over the carpets or finally put away the piles of laundry. The main areas of the home get a once-over, the bedrooms doors get pulled shut, and perhaps the furniture gets dusted.

The one room that probably gets the most attention, however, is the bathroom because, let's face it, it's a room guests are likely to check out. If they're curious, they may even look behind the shower curtain or in the medicine cabinet. But while guests may be checking your bathroom sink for dried toothpaste, your mother is going straight for your secret area of messiness: the microwave.

When Samuel went to Jesse's house looking for the next king, he thought he knew what he was looking for. He had an image in his mind of what a king would look like. So when the first son stood before him in all of his strength and stature, Samuel assumed he must be the one. But the Lord hadn't chosen that son or any of the other seemingly obvious choices.

God wasn't impressed by or put off by any of the sons' outward appearances. The Lord was only concerned with the heart of each man, and He knew that the heart that would follow hard after Him was inside David, the shepherd boy.

Our heavenly Father sees what other people don't. There's no way to hide your mess from Him. No matter how shiny your bathroom may be, He's going to look in the microwave.

Sometimes, Lord, I want to clean myself up for You. I polish the outside in order to appear good enough. You, however, see right to the heart of who I am, and that's a good thing.

LEFTOVERS

But Jesus often withdrew to lonely places and prayed.

LUKE 5:16

Holiday meals are special times when family members are intentional about gathering together around the table. The food is plentiful, and the fellowship is sweet. We enjoy conversation, laughter, and, most importantly, leftovers! When the meal is finished and all of the partially eaten dishes are transferred into storage containers and put in the refrigerator, everyone retires to another room, insisting that they won't be able to eat for days.

Later that evening, however, someone pulls out the leftovers. The ham gets nibbled on, potato salad is scooped out, and a piece of pie and another roll are eaten, as folks are still happy with the day's offerings. But the next day, the meat is a little dry, the macaroni and cheese is long gone, and the deviled eggs have shriveled up in a most unappetizing way. It isn't quite as satisfying. The leftovers have overstayed their welcome.

Sometimes we treat our spiritual lives the same way. We attend worship on Sunday morning, filling ourselves on music and preaching, and we leave the church building feeling full and satisfied. Perhaps it even seems as if we've been fed enough to last the whole week.

The example Jesus set, however, was not a once-a-week trip to a spiritual buffet. Christ worshiped in the synagogue, but He also consistently spent time with God alone, filling Himself with the things of God and encouraging us to do the same. Leftovers are simply not satisfying.

Instill in me, Lord, an insatiable appetite for You. Awaken in me a hunger for Your presence and Your Word.

A WELL-STOCKED PANTRY

*Always be prepared to give an answer to everyone who asks
you to give the reason for the hope that you have.*

1 PETER 3:15

Have you ever had a sudden craving for a certain food, but the only thing in your kitchen was some instant oatmeal, a sleeve of saltines, and a pack of hot dog buns? Or perhaps an unexpected storm came, and you weren't able to leave your house. Those are the times when you realize the pitiful state of your pantry. Being snowed in is no fun without sufficient supplies. ("Supplies" is, of course, code for coffee and chocolate.) It's frustrating not to have what you need when you need it.

When it comes to the spiritual aspect of our lives, however, it's more than frustrating when we find ourselves unprepared; it's dangerous. Scripture tells us that we should *always* be prepared to defend our hope. The Greek word used in 1 Peter 3:15 refers specifically to a verbal defense. Imagine that you were in a conversation with someone, and they had questions regarding your faith. Would you have what you need to respond, or would you be unprepared?

People's pantries may look very different, yet still serve them quite well in an emergency. You may whip up a homemade chocolate cake while someone else is content with peanut butter and a spoon. Likewise, not everyone is pulling from the same spiritual stockpile. One person may have a seminary degree, while someone else is a new believer. That's the beauty of faith. When it comes to defending it, the answer is the same. The reason for our hope is always simply Jesus.

I do not want to be caught unprepared, Lord.
I want your Word in my heart and in my mind so that
when others ask, I can tell them about You.

SHADOWS

Even though I walk through the valley of the shadow of death . . .

If you sit on your front steps as the sun goes down, your imagination can run away with you. A street lamp can look a little eery. The trees may seem a tad sinister. That jacket you draped over the handrail resembles a hunched-over old man coming up your steps. Suddenly, nothing looks familiar. The shadows play tricks on your eyes, and ordinary things appear evil. Then someone flips on the porch light, and you're reminded that it was all just a shadow.

This same scenario plays out in children's bedrooms. A night light casts a stuffed animal's shadow on the wall, causing it to appear far larger and scarier. Moms and dads have to explain that it's only a shadow. With a flip of the light switch, the darkness retreats and what is real remains.

Because of Christ's work on the cross, believers will never feel the sting of death. All that must be endured is a brief walk within its shadow. There's no denying that it can be scary in the shadows, yet we can take comfort in knowing that the *shadow of death* is all that we face. He has delivered us so that we never face the real thing.

Yes, life can be hard. No one can deny the hurt and the heartbreak. But we must remember that we are merely living in the shadows. When Christ returns, He will shine His light, and we'll see everything as it truly is.

The shadows can be a scary place, Lord. Thank You for conquering death so that the shadow of it is all I will ever have to face.

MAMA'S COOKIES

Do not turn from it to the right hand or to the left, that
you may have good success wherever you go.

JOSHUA 1:7 ESV

Sometimes it's okay to be a little creative in the kitchen. Sneak a packet of ranch dressing into your instant mashed potatoes and pass them off as homemade. Substitute cinnamon for cumin in a recipe. Perhaps no one will notice. Some substitutions and shortcuts are the prerogative of every cook.

If you're attempting to recreate your mama's famous cookies, however, following the recipe is key. If she used a whole stick of butter, then that's what you must do as well. If she says to stir nonstop or your work will be for naught, then you'd better stir your little heart out. And if she says to always add more chocolate than the book says, who are you to question it? You don't stray from her recipe because, in the end, you want to be successful in your mission to recreate the perfect cookie.

Following God is a lot like that. In His Word, He has clearly outlined what He wants for your life. He has given instructions on how to interact with others and how to worship Him. Scripture is clear about what is acceptable and what is not. He has shown you what is good (Micah 6:8), and you must simply follow the recipe. To faithfully keep to His teaching is the key to successfully navigating this life.

I have been guilty, Lord, of trying to make substitutions and take
shortcuts. I have tried to do things my way when You have clearly
outlined the right way. Please help me follow Your commandments.

PORCH LIGHT

Jesus spoke to them, saying, "I am the light of the world. Whoever follows me will not walk in darkness, but will have the light of life."

JOHN 8:12 ESV

When you were a teenager, did your parents leave the porch light on for you? Pulling into the driveway and seeing that light signaled that someone was waiting up for you. Someone was looking forward to your safe return.

There's something incredibly comforting about a porch light. A porch light can indicate that someone isn't home, but they will return. It can be a sign to a new visitor that he or she is in the right place. A porch light tells guests that someone is expecting them. It illuminates a walkway so that no one falls. One evening a year, a lit porch light even means that you can knock on someone's door and get candy.

Of all the ways the Son of God could have chosen to describe Himself, Jesus refers to Himself as the Light of the World. Having the light of Jesus in the midst of a dark world brings great comfort. Much like a porch light on a dark evening, the light of Jesus lets us know when we're on the right path. Staying close to His light ensures that we don't go astray.

God has always been about the business of bringing light to His people. From His first act of creation to the sending of His own Son, He has been casting out darkness. No matter how dark the night gets, Scripture assures us that the darkness can never overcome the Light.

Lord, You are the light of my world. I never have to know darkness because of You. Help me to be a light in someone's life, bringing them comfort and pointing them to You.

THE LILY TREE

His mercies never come to an end; they are new every
morning; great is your faithfulness.

LAMENTATIONS 3:22–23 ESV

If you drive down a certain road in a small town in Tennessee, a tree blooms at the edge of a drive. The flowers are a beautiful deep pink, and each year they bloom even prettier than the year before. Any stranger passing by would consider it to be a lovely crepe myrtle tree.

To the couple who planted it, however, it will always be the Lily tree. Lily was to be the second daughter for this young couple. As soon as the pregnancy was confirmed, names were discussed and nursery colors chosen. The child's room would be pink, and her name would be Lily. But the baby the woman held in her womb was never held in her arms. In Lily's memory, the couple planted a tree.

What was meant simply to be a memorial, however, turned into a constant reminder of God's faithfulness. No matter how brutal the winter, that tree blossomed every spring. When it began to grow too large, the man pruned it back, and though the woman feared too much had been trimmed, the next year it bloomed bigger than it ever had before.

One hot July day, the man and woman moved away because God called them to another place. Pulling out of the driveway, they watched as the Lily tree disappeared into the distance, reminding them of a difficult season. One morning, after a particularly sleepless night, the woman received a text from her dad. It said simply, "Lily." Attached was a picture of that tree in all of its beautiful pink glory, and she was reminded that God is forever faithful.

The next time you're out driving around, admiring someone's lovely landscaping, stop for a moment and take it all in. It just might be my Lily tree, and I pray it reminds you of Him.

Lord, You are so faithful. You hold the hurting
and bind up the broken. Even after the darkest
night, You awaken me with mercies anew.

TOUR OF HOMES

Then Saul's son Jonathan came to David in Horesh
and encouraged him in his faith in God.

1 SAMUEL 23:16 HCSB

Have you ever gone on a tour of homes? People open up their profession-
ally decorated houses and allow complete strangers to gawk at their stuff.
Every room is exquisitely decorated, and nothing is out of place. Let's just say
that they don't just ask any ol' homeowners to participate in the tour.

Now, imagine yourself walking up to the owner of one of those beautiful
homes and offering some improvements on the decor. Perhaps you could sug-
gest some fingerprints on the glass for a more lived-in look. Everyone these days
is adding a pop of color, choosing a colorful throw or decorative pillow. Maybe
you could share your secret for achieving surprise pops of color: grape juice
stains on the carpet. Obviously, you wouldn't really do this, assuming that they
would not need your home decorating advice.

Sadly, many believers view other believers as if they were on the tour of
Christ-followers. Whether it's your pastor's wife or someone else you really
respect, you feel inadequate to offer spiritual encouragement. The fact is, however, everyone needs someone to be a source of encouragement.

David was a man after God's own heart. From his youth, he was God's
anointed one. Yet, in a season of suffering, his friend Jonathan encouraged
him in his faith. Even the man after God's own heart needed someone to give
his faith a boost.

Don't let the enemy rob you of a chance to encourage someone else. No one
is 100 percent sure of themselves all of the time. Everyone enters seasons of

doubt and struggle. Don't be afraid to walk up to people you respect and remind them that God is in control.

Open my eyes, Lord, to opportunities to be an encouragement to those around me. Don't let me see anyone as too spiritual for me to approach.

TELEPHONE CONVERSATIONS

Do not be hasty to speak, and do not be impulsive to make a speech before God. God is in heaven and you are on earth, so let your words be few.

ECCLESIASTES 5:2 HCSB

Have you ever been on the phone with someone and the signal was lost? Did it take you several minutes to realize that the person was no longer listening? Sometimes it's easy to get so wrapped up in what we're saying that we don't even notice that there's no response from the other end. It's kind of embarrassing, isn't it?

Or perhaps you tend to interrupt others. Your friend says something that reminds you of something else, and without warning, you change the subject. Do you find yourself later realizing that your friend never finished her story?

Sadly, our prayer lives sometimes resemble a one-sided phone conversation. We begin by telling God all of the things that we think we need. We outline for Him exactly how we're going to carry out His plans for our lives—and we don't always ask Him what those plans are! On we go, full-steam ahead, without realizing that we haven't heard a response from God. We are so busy talking that God's silence slips right past us.

Other times we begin to get a vision for something God wants us to do. But before He can finish preparing us or outlining His plan, we rush off with only half of the story. It may be a good idea for us to slow down just a little.

When we pause to spend time with God, we don't need to be quick to start talking. God knows our hearts, and He doesn't need so many of our words. Our friends would probably appreciate a little more listening too.

Teach me, Lord, to be quick to listen and slow to speak. I do not want to miss anything that You want to say to me.

THE WELCOME MAT

Turn to me and be gracious to me, for I am lonely and afflicted.

PSALM 25:16

A welcome mat on a front porch makes an entire house seem friendly. The people stepping onto the mat feel invited into that space. Before the front door even opens, they're officially welcomed into the home. The world could use a few more welcome mats.

Women who are lonely are everywhere. They are laundry-folding, nose-wiping, boo-boo-kissing, grilled cheese-making machines. They are single ladies, working nine to five and swapping jokes around the water cooler. Church volunteers, classroom moms, and doting grandmothers—they are all ages and in all life stages, and they are lonely.

What can you do to make a difference in a lonely woman's life? You can roll out the welcome mat and invite her into your space. It's okay if you have toys on the floor and peanut butter smeared on the kitchen counter. Let her bring her loneliness and sit with you in the midst of your laundry piles while *Dora the Explorer* plays in the background. Don't feel the pressure first to clean up your mess. Make her feel welcome, and help her see that she isn't as alone as she thought.

People don't necessarily need someone who can fix their problems. They aren't always looking for someone who understands every little thing they're currently going through. Sometimes all they need is to know that they are welcome and that they don't have to leave their mess at the door. When we roll out the welcome mat, we may be surprised by who has been waiting for someone to invite them in.

Lord, teach me the art of loving people well by welcoming them into my home. Make my home a place where they can feel loved and wanted when they enter and a little less lonely when they leave.

A SUPERMARKET STORY

Everyone watched as they made their way around the store. She pushed his wheelchair and pulled her buggy all at the same time. At one point, she left him sitting by the frozen foods as she went to look for an item. That's when it happened. Without warning, his body arched and his head fell back. He began convulsing, and people started murmuring, "It's a seizure."

Although some knew exactly what to do in that situation, others stood there horrified and holding a frozen pie crust. A crowd gathered and some began to offer assistance, but the woman waved them away. Very calmly, she picked the man's hat up off the floor and placed it on his head. She patted his shoulder and said, "It's okay. I'm here, just like always."

There are times in life when we encounter scary situations. What should have been an ordinary day turns into something unexpected and unwanted. Someone gets ill or injured; a relationship ends; a job is lost. It's easy to panic. Fear clouds our vision, and we forget that we are not alone.

God is always by our side. He never gets tired of walking with us and never grows weary of doing the heavy lifting when we are weak. He is never embarrassed by our frailty or annoyed by our weakness. When others don't know how to help, He is there. When friends walk away, He stays. Wherever we find ourselves when trouble comes, God will be there, just like always.

There have been seasons, Lord, when I could not have taken a single step without You. You have been more faithful than friends and more constant than family. Thank You for never leaving me.

HOT CUP OF COFFEE

And they sat with him on the ground seven days and seven nights, and no one spoke a word to him, for they saw that his suffering was very great.

JOB 2:13 ESV

When someone is hurting or struggling, it's natural to want to lend a hand. Church folks are great at organizing help in all sorts of ways. Are you having a baby? Is someone in your family ill? Just let the ladies in your church know, and within no time they will have a lasagna and some lemon bars delivered to your door. People will mow your lawn, bring you groceries, and watch your children. We are a society of doers, which can be a good thing. However, there are times when even the most sincere offering cannot make the situation better.

Oftentimes nothing can be done, and the best way to help is to just be present. For all that Job's friends may have done wrong, they got this part right. When they heard of all the tragedies Job had endured, they decided to show up. They couldn't fix anything, and they didn't presume to know how he felt. They simply sat with him in silence.

Sometimes hurting people just need your presence, to sit and drink a cup of coffee with no words spoken. Sometimes all people need is a moment when they're not obligated to share all the details and you're not pressured to offer advice. When there's nothing to be said, don't say a thing. A chance to breathe and a friend's presence can be two of the most healing things.

Lord, help me learn the ministry of simply being present in someone's pain. Teach me to put aside my own discomfort or need to fix things and simply offer silence and coffee.

SURVIVING GOOD-BYE

There is nothing on earth that I desire besides you.

PSALM 73:25 ESV

There was a time when folks lived and died in the same small town. It wasn't uncommon to grow up right down the road from grandparents. You would never dare to act out in public because everyone knew your family. These days people rarely live their whole lives without pulling up roots and replanting themselves somewhere new. Most of us have lived a lifetime of good-byes.

No matter how much we wish it were different, good-byes are a part of life. Circumstances change. People change. Life happens. Jobs change, and friendships end. Sometimes we must leave people and places that are dear to our hearts. Other times those we love leave us. Good-byes are rarely happy and often are painful.

Through it all, we must learn to hold on very loosely to the things of this life. The things and people we cherish must be held with open hands rather than closed fists, as we entrust them to the One who loves them even more. We can trust Him to restore joy and redeem pain.

Wanting the Lord more than we want anything or anyone else is the key to surviving good-bye. He must be our heart's greatest desire. If God calls us to a good-bye, He can bring good from it. If it's painful, we can trust that He will use it for His glory. Yes, we will hurt, and we will grieve. But at the end of the day, He will heal.

I have said so many good-byes, Lord. I have had to let go of people I thought would never leave. But I trust You, Jesus, to create beauty from the ashes of my good-byes.

PLAYING IN THE SNOW

Put on the whole armor of God, that you may be able
to stand against the schemes of the devil.

EPHESIANS 6:11 ESV

If you live anywhere that sees a fair amount of snow during the winter, then you're probably aware of the importance of snow gear. Any true northerner knows that you don't simply rush out in freezing temperatures to make a snow angel in your front yard. There are a series of items that you must first put on your body. A warm sweater is needed to hold in body heat. A properly insulated jacket keeps out the cold. Appropriate footwear is needed to prevent wet feet.

At this point, you may feel prepared to take on the frigid temperatures; however, you aren't fully protected. You still must wrap a scarf around your neck, put a hat on your head, and pull gloves onto your hands. Only then are you ready to step out and face Old Man Winter.

It may be tempting, in the rush to get on with things, to skip one of these items. The problem, however, is that each item protects a certain part of the body. Each one has its own job, and without it, you'll be vulnerable to the cold.

When Paul wrote his letter to the Ephesians, he told them how they could defend themselves against the devil. He carefully listed each item they needed to properly protect themselves: belt of truth, breastplate of righteousness, shield of faith, helmet of salvation, shoes of peace, and sword of the Spirit. In one short passage, Paul told the believers to put on the *whole* armor of God. To neglect any part of the armor would be to leave some area vulnerable to the enemy's attack.

You wouldn't rush out to make a snowman with your bare hands, nor would you trudge through the snow wearing flip-flops. You wouldn't go out in the snow without being properly protected. How much more important, then, is it to be properly protected before going out into the world?

Lord, You have provided what I need to defend myself against the attacks of the enemy. Give me wisdom to don each item before stepping out into the world each day.

CHRISTMAS LIGHTS

"You are the light of the world. A town built on a hill cannot be hidden."

MATTHEW 5:14

No one loves Christmas more than my dad. My parents had a way of making it magical every year, and a huge part of that experience was the decorating. There was only one kind of Christmas tree to buy: the biggest one we could find. And there was only one place to put our humongous Christmas tree: in front of the biggest window in our home.

My dad decorated with the neighbors and passersby in mind, and his joy came from seeing others enjoying his work. I have many memories of going outside, in the dark and cold, to make sure that our tree looked as good from the road as it did from the living room. There could never be too many ornaments or too many lights. In fact, if the house couldn't be seen from a mile away, it just wasn't lit up enough.

When Jesus teaches that we, as His followers, are to be the light of the world, I picture our house all lit up on Christmas Eve. The light of our faith is not for our benefit only. There are too many people living in darkness for us to selfishly hide our light. In fact, Jesus says that a town built on a hill *cannot* be hidden. The implication is that, if we are filled with the light of Jesus, we are unable to keep it hidden. We can't help but illuminate the paths of those around us. The light of our faith should be as evident from the road as it is from our living room.

Lord, it was never Your intention that I hoard Your light for myself. Help me to step out of my comfort zone and seek to brighten some of the darkness around me.

GIFTS

Having gifts that differ according to the grace given to us, let us use them.

Romans 12:6 ESV

Many women have bought into the lie that there is a right way and a wrong way to do everything. Often we are unable to acknowledge the gifts in another woman without feeling envious of her or disgusted with ourselves. The fact is that we all have different gifts. Your gifts are not better, and mine are not worse; they're just different.

Whether you monogram your baby's cloth diapers or run each morning while pushing a toddler in a jogging stroller and munching on homemade granola, we all have specific gifts. We can find freedom in acknowledging our differences—and freedom feels good.

Along with the acknowledgment that we all possess gifts is the assumption that we will actually use our gifts. We were each given a specific gift for a specific purpose. Perhaps the purpose benefits you. The reality is, however, that our gifts are often for the benefit of others. Consider the gifts Paul lists: prophecy, service, teaching, encouragement, generosity, leadership, and mercy. Each of these gifts is a blessing to those on the receiving end.

The enemy will try to convince us not to use our gifts. He might even try to get us to deny that we have any. We may call it humility, but it's actually selfish to hoard our gifts, which were given to us to benefit the people God has placed in our lives. So let's go out and use the gifts we've been given.

Forgive me for not using the gifts You have given me for Your glory.
Reveal to me my gifts, and give me the boldness to use them.

CHANGE OF PLANS

In the sixth month the angel Gabriel was sent from God to a city of Galilee named Nazareth, to a virgin betrothed to a man whose name was Joseph.

LUKE 1:26–27 ESV

Have you ever planned an elaborate dinner party only to have your guests cancel? Or spent days anticipating a date with your spouse only to have the babysitter get sick? It's so disappointing when the best-laid plans go awry.

Women are a planning sort of people. As a whole, we tend to be less of the go-with-the-flow type. We plan births, meals, and wardrobes with great attention to detail. We research and analyze things to death. With that in mind, how can you not have compassion for Mary? The girl was planning a marriage.

Maybe she was deciding what entrée to serve and arranging seating to make sure Aunt Bertha didn't sit too close to the wine table, or maybe she was writing "Mary loves Joseph" in the dirt with a stick. Scripture makes it clear that when Gabriel showed up, Mary was a betrothed woman. She surely had some things planned, and those plans did not include giving birth to the Son of God.

We've all had times when our plans didn't work out. Perhaps we thought we would be married by now, yet our Facebook status still reads "single." Or we always assumed we would *still* be married right now. We imagined ourselves with a flourishing career, but instead we find ourselves eking out a minimum-wage existence.

We thought we would be doing something else, be with someone else, *be* someone else. But God had other plans.

Our mistake is that we want to compare our plan with God's plan. We want to see them side by side and weigh the pros and cons of each. Our best response, however, will always be the same as Mary's when the angel crashed her wedding plans. "Let it be to me according to your word" (Luke 1:38 ESV).

Lord, I like to think that I have everything planned out. Remind me to always leave room in my plans for Your providence.

RAIN PUDDLES

For God gave us a spirit not of fear but of power and love and self-control.

2 TIMOTHY 1:7 ESV

Kids are drawn to rain puddles. Something about a pool of water, no matter how small, seems to beckon little feet to play. As adults, though, most of us will attempt to navigate around the puddles. We will walk out of our way to avoid getting our shoes wet. Perhaps we'll even choose to stay on the porch and avoid the rain altogether. Children, however, march bravely right through.

Life can be a lot like a driveway after a heavy rain. There will be potholes and puddles. And chances are, no matter how hard we try, our feet will get wet. We have options, of course. We can stand on the porch and not venture out at all for fear of ruining our shoes. We can walk, timidly and slowly, down the drive in an attempt to stay dry. Or we can learn a little something from children.

We can kick off our shoes and run boldly down the driveway, choosing not to be afraid because God didn't create us to live that way. We can accept the fact that there will be some puddles that we can avoid and some we cannot. And we may be surprised to discover that some puddles, which we thought were obstacles, were actually gifts.

God didn't create us to sit on the porch forever. Sure, it's safe and dry. Sometimes, however, He calls us to run down the driveway. He asks us to march bravely through the puddles. No child ever regretted splashing in a rain puddle, and no Christ-follower ever regretted a life spent boldly following Him.

I have spent too much time, Lord, being timid. Fear has caused me to miss out on the joy of being used by You. Thank You for the reminder that fear never comes from You. Teach me the beauty of boldness.

Let the peace of God's creation lift your soul as you experience powerful devotions from your favorite places. *Devotions for the Beach* and *Devotions from the Garden* will remind you of God's constant presence and bring inspiration to your daily life.